Prophe

Prophecies

and other Literary Writings

Leonardo da Vinci

Translated by J.G. Nichols

ET REMOTISSIMA PROPE

100 PAGES

100 PAGES
Published by Hesperus Press Limited
4 Rickett Street, London SW6 1RU
www.hesperuspress.com

First published by Hesperus Press Limited, 2002

Introduction and English language translation © J.G. Nichols, 2002
Foreword © Eraldo Affinati, 2002

Designed and typeset by Fraser Muggeridge
Printed in the United Arab Emirates by Oriental Press

ISBN: 1-84391-016-0

CONTENTS

FOREWORD

Everyone recognises Leonardo as the greatest artist of his time: without him our feeling for the Italian landscape, for instance, would be quite different. But who was Leonardo the writer? We could think of him as an active scientist, an explorer of the universe fascinated by the multifarious and never-ending transformations of Nature, with his notebook in his pocket. A humanist with a poet's heart who seems to foreshadow the experimental method of Galileo. His lack of a formal education prevented him from fully mastering Latin, but also drove him to argue with those who blindly accepted the established beliefs of the ancients. Leonardo da Vinci was left-handed: he wrote from right to left, so that his text became legible when reflected in a mirror. His fragments, which have come down to us despite innumerable vicissitudes, add up to about seven thousand sheets of paper, distributed throughout ancient codices, with fascinating titles: *Atlantic*, *Trivulziano*, *Arundel*, *Forster*, *Flight of Birds*. They were published in the nineteenth and twentieth centuries in Milan, Paris, London, and Turin.

The illegitimate child of Piero, a notary, Leonardo developed his versatile genius working from his childhood in the studio of Andrea Verrocchio in Florence, side by side with famous painters and sculptors. He never forgot his humble origins: in his 'Pleasantries' – accounts of talk and merriment with his friends, including many jokes – we read the dialogue between two people, one of whom accuses the other of being illegitimate. The latter replies that, according to natural law, whoever throws such an insult in someone else's face when he is not entitled to, is the illegitimate one, since he is himself behaving like a beast.

To read Leonardo's codices is to achieve a real, genuine

'return to the future', thanks to the number of discoveries he made, both little and great. His writings, although influenced by the Neoplatonic climate of opinion, originate in something new in Italian culture: there is no trace of the show-case or the monastery or the library. No ink is used, no magnifying glass held over the page. The author lives out of doors, in the open, and with a pencil he notes down what he observes in the sky: 'The moon, dense and heavy, dense and heavy, how is it with the moon?'

For Leonardo, who was keen to exalt his condition of unlettered man, calling himself '*omo sanza lettere*', what was important was the suggestive power of words, which were conceived not as a simple communication tool but rather as the voice of human conscience. His desire to know and experiment lends his prose an almost feverish tension – at the same time lyrical and rational, tangible and suggestive – which requires both a logical and emotional involvement from the modern reader. His 'Prophecies' are disguised riddles that were recited by the great artist, in the role of soothsayer or prophet, at the Court of Ludovico, known as the Moor. So fire transforms one thing into another, tinder makes visible what turns out to have been hidden, Christians believe in the Son and build temples in the name of His Mother. Often these riddles seem to allude to tragic and mysterious events in the future, but after first scaring the audience, they make them smile. His moral intention shows up unmistakably through descriptions that appear to challenge painting to single combat. So the dead become birds that assail men by pecking at their food, and the waves of the sea rise to the sky where they long remain in the shape of clouds. With Leonardo image replaces discourse, as if he were aware that words are not so expressive as painting. But it is this very sense of inadequacy that makes his writings so fascinating.

The 'Fables' are perhaps Leonardo's finest achievement from the point of view of style: he wrote them for the dignitaries who invited him to court but, far from considering them mere commissions, he saw them as ingenious syntheses of his thought. The butterfly which, irresistibly attracted by the light of a flame, dies in passing through it, and the monkey which, enamoured of a bird, suffocates it with kisses, are typical examples of such intentions: whoever does not recognise Nature's laws, as they relate to himself or to others, is destined to fail. Some years later he would note down in his 'Thoughts': 'Those who are enamoured of practice without knowledge are like pilots who embark without a helm or compass, and never know for certain where they are going.'

The 'Bestiary' demonstrates this profound respect for the harmony of the cosmos, where every animal has precise characteristics: we find thieving partridges, eagles which are generous because *noblesse oblige*, foxes which are quick-change artistes, falcons which are solitary and proud, lustful bats, hypocritical crocodiles, indomitable panthers.

When we read these writings, we have to remember that their fragmentary nature is not just due to practical circumstances. Leonardo always started from the particular in order to rise to the universal, using a concise, incisive, aphoristic style, as he pencilled down quick annotations in small notebooks that he later copied randomly on larger sheets. Scholars have described this method as 'particled composition'. However, this does not prevent us from linking all the available documents with the world-view they originated from. Only then will these texts reflect, even in their provisional and disarranged structure, an extraordinary idea of life.

Leonardo wonders about the origin of the motion which makes Nature take this or that form, passing from one form to another, in an incessant process of lithe and luminous splendour, and changing bodies and matter without ever fixing them permanently, visible and invisible at the same time, like a ball of opaque glass. The work of Marsilio Ficino, who made a Christian synthesis of Aristotle, Pythagoras, and Plato, was perhaps an influence on him; in any case, Leonardo never stopped taking account of real tangible events. He was aware of the practical value of experiments, while at the same time, as a poet, he lived with the sense of what is inaccessible and mysterious beyond such limits: 'Nature is full of infinite causes which have never been found out by experiment.' And again: 'There is no effect in Nature without a cause. Understand the cause, and you will have no need of experience.'

The 'wonderful inevitability' of the universe shines through the face of Mona Lisa and inspires man with a sense of wonder which makes him trust in God. The great artist attacks those who try to change universal laws – especially alchemists and necromancers. 'His conversation was so pleasing that he drew men's hearts to him,' wrote Vasari. We may well believe it. Leonardo was much more a part of human society than were many of the writers and artists who preceded him. Isolated, but certainly not estranged from the culture of his time, he points out to all of us his way towards a total humanism, bound up as it was with the condition of his own peers, and yet capable of creating masterpieces: 'Just as a day well spent brings happy sleep, so a life well employed brings a happy death.' From him we can also learn both the sense of action as a healthy thing and the secret dignity of existence: 'One cannot have greater lordship, or lesser lordship, than over oneself.' This was the pride of the Renaissance.

– Eraldo Affinati, 2002

INTRODUCTION

This book contains only a selection of Leonardo's writings; and those writings are themselves fragmentary, and the fragments are often tantalisingly brief. In this respect at least, then, this book is fairly representative of the work of the great scientist, artist, and engineer: he was always famous for initiating more projects than he could possibly complete. However, frustrating as this may be, it is also part of his charm. The reader must be prepared for mystery. If we think, for instance, of his paintings, it would be difficult to maintain that his *Mona Lisa* is a better, a more complex and satisfying work than, say, his *Annunciation* now in Florence's Uffizi Gallery. And yet the *Mona Lisa* is much more widely known – indeed probably the best known – of all Leonardo's works, because we have to wonder what the lady is smiling at, or even if she is actually smiling, or… She, like Leonardo, leaves us guessing.

Similarly, we are often uncertain as to the exact significance of Leonardo's writings. We cannot always be sure of the tone of his voice. He does make jokes – and not only in the section headed 'Pleasantries' – but, owing largely to the fragmentary nature of these writings, the twinkle in the eye which writers can sometimes convey every bit as well as painters is not always obvious.

Two things, however, are obvious: his thoughts are always exploratory, and usually moral. He is a wonderful example of the truth of the Platonic maxim that 'the unexamined life is no fit life for a human being'. We are creatures who have an innate need to understand things, and Leonardo would have agreed with Dante's Ulysses who, even in Hell, recalls making the same point to his old companions in order to urge them to undertake their last, disastrous voyage:

Consider where you come from: from your birth
Not meant to live like beasts, but to pursue
Virtue and understanding here on earth.
(Inferno 26, 118-20)

By 'moral' I do not mean – how could I? – that his thoughts are always such as one can approve of. I mean that when he sees a problem (and Leonardo is fundamentally a man who sees problems everywhere) it usually has some relevance to the way human beings ought to act. The teasing quality in Leonardo's writings – which is sometimes deliberate, and sometimes an accidental result of the process of time – should not distract us, as it did not distract him, from his fundamental concern with 'virtue and understanding'.

All these features are clear in the first section, 'Prophecies'. The language here is often oracular, as though the writer has something important to impart, and the sayings could often be read as genuine attempts to prophesy. But he does not only give us prophecies, in the mysterious and often riddling language which prophets love to use, but he also tells us what the prophecies mean. This is not part of the traditional role of the prophet. Indeed, this is precisely what serious prophets avoid doing. The sixteenth-century French prophet, Nostradamus, owes his continuing fame to the fact that his prophecies are couched in language, always vague and frequently meta-phorical, which demands interpretation and can always be interpreted in such a way that the prophecies appear to come true. Nowadays the writers of horoscopes in newspapers work on the same principle, although usually without the lurid tropes of Nostradamus. We may be told, say, that we can 'expect trouble midweek'. Of course we can: trouble of some sort there always is and always will be. Leonardo's inclusion of the solutions (the word is reasonable, because so many of the prophecies sound like riddles) turns his prophecies into a mockery of human attempts, or pretensions, to prophesy. Including the solutions with the prophecies even suggests at times that Leonardo is offering recipes: everyone, he seems to be implying, can be his own prophet if he just learns the tricks. In this satirical, and therefore moral, intention Leonardo is in the same tradition as Jonathan Swift more than two centuries later. Swift dealt his blow to prophesying by making a prophecy himself. He announced that one of his contemporaries, Partridge, a man who had pretensions to foretelling the future, would die on a certain date. Then, on that date, Swift announced that his prophecy had been fulfilled. So Partridge was left in the unenviable position of having to persuade people he was still alive – something he found much more difficult than foretelling the future.

This does not exhaust the meaning of Leonardo's 'Prophecies'. Sometimes they open up other fields for thought and discovery, and leave us turning over in the mind things which we may previously have taken for granted:

> 'Men will be treated with great pomp and ceremony, without their knowledge. [*Of funerals, their services and processions and lights and bells and company.*]'

Sometimes they can be remarkable in their wisdom:

> 'Men will pursue what they fear the most. [*That is, they will live in poverty in order to avoid poverty.*]'

That this is wise, as well as witty, reminds us that the categories into which these writings are put are not necessarily mutually exclusive, and some prophecies could well be included in, for instance, 'Thoughts and Aphorisms', among such sayings as this:

'He who wishes to get rich in a day is hanged in a year.'

While the exposing of charlatans and all their chicanery is clearly a moral act, it is difficult to claim such a prestigious intention for many of Leonardo's 'Pleasantries'. The longer anecdotes have some of the sharpness of Boccaccio, but the shorter jokes seem no more than diversions from more serious occupations, and a reminder that, just as 'Good poets have a weakness for bad puns', so they often enjoy silly jokes. I am reminded of Ben Jonson, whose preoccupations in his writings were every bit as serious and moral as Leonardo's. The record of Jonson's conversations with Drummond of Hawthornden in 1619 contains, among much shrewd literary and other criticism, such gems as the following:

'What is that, the more you [take] out of it, groweth still the longer? A ditch.'

And yet, it is too easy to sneer. Such riddles and jokes require – not only to solve them but even merely to enjoy them – the same kind of lateral thinking which can lead to more weighty results. It was necessary to look at things in a sidelong, unexpected way in order to write *Volpone*, in Jonson's case, and in order to think ahead to, say, submarines and helicopters in Leonardo's.

With the 'Bestiary' we see a strange mingling of interests. Sometimes Leonardo is simply fascinated by what is exotic. However, many of the creatures are included in order to be allegorised. This is particularly obvious when the quality they stand for is put before the description of the creature itself:

> '*Magnanimity*. The falcon only preys upon big birds, and it would sooner die than feed on little birds or stinking meat.'

Sometimes Leonardo's interest is what we can recognise as scientific: we gather that he would rather like to anatomise the creatures physically if he could. And there is one obvious reason for these three different approaches. Some of the creatures (like cicadas) must have been quite familiar to Leonardo, others (like elephants) less familiar or even known only from reliable hearsay, and still others (like the two-headed amphisboena or the crocodile-killing ichneumon) quite impossible for him to have seen.

If the 'Bestiary' tends to show Leonardo at his most 'medieval', concerned more with tradition than observed fact, and more anxious to allegorise than analyse, then his 'Fragments of a Spiritual Autobiography' reveal more of what we think of as the modern approach – the Renaissance emphasis on observation and discovery rather than on authority. He says that his 'ideas are simply the result of experience – the true teacher', and he mocks the medieval insistence on always backing up one's ideas by referring, and deferring, to authority:

> 'He who in disputes brings authority to bear is not using his mind but his memory.'

This clash between a scientific approach and the older, more traditional, appeal to longstanding habits of mind was evident in Leonardo's day in the question of using dead bodies (often, and significantly, those of criminals) for the study of human anatomy. It is perhaps a symptom of Leonardo's greatness that he can give due weight to both points of view while siding with the moderns:

> 'O investigator of this anatomy of ours, do not be saddened by the fact that your knowledge is bought with someone else's death, but rejoice that our Creator has concentrated your mind on such an excellent instrument.'

And it is another, and no less important, symptom of his greatness that in his 'Fragments of a Spiritual Autobiography', as so often elsewhere in this work, he includes the occasional tart remark – an implicit reminder that exploration in the pursuit of truth does not oblige us to leave our sense of humour at home:

> 'I do not meddle with royal decrees, because they are the perfection of truth.'

– J. G. Nichols, 2002

Prophecies

Something will appear which will cover whoever tries to cover it. [*The sun's rays hitting a surface.*]

From deep caverns he will come who will make all the peoples of the world toil and sweat, with great trouble, labour, and anxiety, so that they may have his help. [*Of gold and the money made from it.*]

That which is evil and dreadful will strike such fear of itself into men that, almost as though they were mad, they will, believing that they are fleeing from it, swiftly feel its immeasurable force. [*Of the fear of poverty.*]

And he who is most necessary to the one who has need of him, will be unknown, and once known, the more despised. [*Of advice.*]

There is something which, the more it is needed, the more it is refused. And this is advice, most unwillingly listened to by those who need it, that is the ignorant. There is something which, the more you fear it and flee from it, the nearer it comes to you. And this is poverty which, the more you flee from it, the more poor and troubled it makes you. [*Of advice and poverty.*]

In the highest reaches of the air long serpents will be seen fighting with birds. [*Of snakes in the beaks of storks.*]

From underground they will come who will deafen the bystanders with fearful shouts, and with their breath cause men to die, and bring down castles and towns. [*Of cannon from pits and moulds.*]

Many, whose faith is in the son, only raise temples in the mother's name. [*Of Christians.*]

Many living bodies will pass through the bodies of other creatures. That is to say, uninhabited houses will pass in pieces through inhabited houses, giving them something useful, and bringing with themselves their own harm. This is to say, man's life is made up of things which are eaten, and they bring with them the part of the man which is dead. [*Of food that was once alive.*]

Men will sleep and eat and dwell among trees which grow in the woods and fields. [*Of men who sleep on boards.*]

It will seem to men that they see strange destruction in the sky. It will look as though flames fly up into the sky and flee in terror down from it. They will hear all kinds of creatures speaking in the language of men. In their bodies they will rush off into various parts of the world, without moving. They will see enormous splendours in the dark. O marvel of the human race, what delirium has brought you to this? You will talk with all kinds of creatures, and they will talk with you, in the language of men. You will see yourself falling from great heights without any harm, with torrents accompanying you in your fall. [*Of dreaming.*]

Many will be those peoples who will hide themselves and their children and their victuals within dark caverns. And there, in those dark holes, they will feed themselves and their families for many months, without any artificial or natural light. [*Of ants.*]

And from many others their provisions and food will be taken, and people will plunge them into water or drown them, pitilessly and without cause. O justice of God, why are you not aroused to see your creatures so ill-used? [*Of bees.*]

Many will have their little ones taken from them and slaughtered and cruelly quartered. [*Of sheep, cows, goats, and the like.*]

With merciless blows many little children will be taken from the arms of their mothers and thrown to the ground and then torn to pieces. [*Of walnuts and olives and acorns and chestnuts and the like.*]

O cities on the shore! I see your citizens, male and female, with their arms and legs tightly bound in heavy bonds by people who do not understand their language. You will only be able to give vent to your grief for your lost liberty by means of pitiful tears and sighs and lamentation one with another, for those who bind you will not understand you, and neither will you understand them. [*Of children who are wrapped in swaddling bands.*]

Cities of Africa, your children will be seen to be torn apart in their own homes by pitiless and rapacious creatures of your own land. [*Of mice and the cats which eat them.*]

O negligent Nature, why are you so biased, acting like a merciful and benign mother to some of your sons, and to others like a cruel and pitiless stepmother? I see your children delivered into slavery, with no benefit to them, and instead of remuneration for the benefits they confer, being repaid with severe sufferings, and always spending their lives for the benefit of those who ill-treat them. [*Of donkeys being beaten.*]

Men will be treated with great pomp and ceremony, without their knowledge. [*Of funerals, their services and processions and lights and bells and company.*]

A wretch will be mocked, and his mockers will always be his deceivers and robbers and assassins. [*Of the municipality.*]

There is something which, however much you take from it, will never lose any of its grandeur. [*The light of a candle.*]

Something else which, the closer you get to it, the more unpleasant and harmful it is. [*Fire.*]

All the astrologers will be castrated. [*That is the cockerels. Of prophecy.*]

There will be many who will move against each other, holding sharp iron in their hands. These will do no harm to each other, except to tire each other out, because whenever one goes forward the other will go back. But woe betide him who places himself in the middle, for in the end he shall be cut to pieces. [*Of sawyers.*]

The mournful shouts will be heard, and the loud cries, the hoarse and feeble voices of those who will be tortured and despoiled and left at the end naked and motionless: and this will be the motive of the driving force which directs everything. [*The spinning-wheel for silk.*]

In every city and land and castle, village and house, the desire to eat will cause food to be taken from the mouth of one and put into the mouth of another, without any resistance. [*Of putting bread in and taking it out of the mouth of an oven.*]

We shall see the earth turned upside down, and look at the opposite hemisphere, and discover the dens of ferocious beasts. [*Tilling the earth.*]

Many of the men who remain alive will throw out of their houses the victuals they have saved, giving them up as prey to the birds of the air and the beasts of the field, taking no care of them at all. [*Of sowing.*]

One will come from the sky who will carry a large part of Africa under that sky towards Europe, and part of Europe towards Africa, and the provincial areas will be mingled in a great revolution. [*Of rain, which makes the muddied rivers carry lands away.*]

In the end earth will turn red after many days' burning, and stones will be changed into ash. [*Of brick-kilns and lime.*]

The trees and shrubs of great forests will turn to ash. [*Of timber which burns.*]

Water creatures will die in boiling waters. [*Boiled fish.*]

He who will give us nourishment and light will come down in a rush from the sky. [*Olives which fall from the trees and give us oil to provide light.*]

Many will perish of broken heads, and their eyes will start from their heads, because of fearful creatures which issue from the shadows. [*Of owls by which birds are limed.*]

His precepts will be revered, honoured, and listened to with reverence and love who was once scorned, torn, and tortured with many blows. [*Of linen whose rags make paper.*]

Bodies without souls will, with their judgements, give us rules teaching us how to die well. [*Of books which teach rules.*]

Men will hide under the skin of stripped grasses, and there, shouting, they will torture themselves, beating their own limbs. [*Of flagellants.*]

They will go mad for the most beautiful things, seeking to possess them and make use of their most ugly parts, and then, with penitence for the harm they have done, and having come to their senses, they will be very pleased with themselves. [*Of lust.*]

Many will they be who, with all zeal and care and haste, will pursue that which has always frightened them, not realising its malignity. [*Of the miser.*]

It will be seen that those who are reputed to be experienced and judicious, the less need they have of things, the more greedily they try to get them and keep them. [*Of men who, the older they grow, the more miserly they become, when – having only a little while to stay – they should be generous.*]

Many will be engaged in the business of taking away from that thing which grows as much as is taken from it. [*Of a ditch. Say it as though in a delirium or raving, as a madman.*]

Of many bodies it will be seen that, when the head is taken from them, they clearly grow, and, when the head is restored, they straightway diminish. [*Of cushions when weight is placed upon them.*]

There will be many hunters of creatures which, the more they catch, the fewer they will have. Conversely, the more they have, the fewer they will catch. [*Of catching lice.*]

And many will keep themselves occupied in this way: the more they draw something up, the more it will flee from them in the opposite direction. [*Of drawing water with two buckets on one rope.*]

Many will make homes for themselves in entrails and live in their own entrails. [*Sausages which are put into entrails.*]

Oh, what a filthy thing, when one animal will be seen to have its tongue in another's arse. [*The tongues of pigs and heifers in entrails.*]

Animals' food will be seen to pass into their skin in every part except through the mouth and come through the other side until it reaches the ground. [*Of sieves made out of animal skins.*]

The fierce horns of powerful bulls will defend nocturnal light from the wild fury of the winds.[1] [*Of lanterns.*]

Men will be borne up on the feathers of flying creatures. [*Of feather beds.*]

The mud will be so deep that men will walk above the trees in their villages. [*Men who wear wooden clogs.*]

And through much of the country people will be seen walking on the skins of great beasts. [*Of the soles of shoes which are made of oxhide.*]

There will be great winds by which eastern things will become western, and southern things, largely mingled with the course of the winds, will follow them for great distances. [*Of navigation.*]

Men will speak to men who cannot hear them; their eyes will be open, but they will not see. They will speak to them and not be answered. They will beg favours of those who have ears but will not hear. They will put light in front of those who are blind. [*Of pictures of venerated saints.*]

Men will walk and not move, speak with people who are not there, and hear someone who does not speak. [*Of dreaming.*]

Shapes and forms of men and animals will be seen, following those animals and men wherever they flee. And the movement of one will be like the movement of the other, but it will be marvellous how their size will change. [*Of a man's shadow which moves with him.*]

Often one man will be seen to become three, and they all follow him; and often the more sure and certain one abandons him. [*Of shadows cast by the sun and seeing oneself mirrored in water at the same time.*]

Huge treasures will be found hidden within walnut trees and other trees. [*Of coffers in which many treasures are kept.*]

Many, by breathing out too quickly, will lose their eyesight and shortly all their feelings. [*Of blowing out the light when going to bed.*]

In many parts of Europe instruments of various sizes will be heard making different harmonies, to the great weariness of those who hear them close by. [*Of mules' bells which are placed near to their ears.*]

Great efforts will be rewarded with hunger, thirst, discomfort, and blows and stings and curses and rudeness. [*Of asses.*]

Many will be seen carried at great speed by huge animals to the ruin of their lives and a very early death. Animals of different colours will be seen carrying men in a frenzy through the air and on the earth to the destruction of their lives. [*Of soldiers on horseback.*]

Men will be seen to go as fast, by means of the stars, as any other rapid creature. [*Of the stars on spurs.*]

The movement of the dead will make people flee with pain and grief, with many lively cries. [*A stick, which is dead.*]

With stone and iron things will be made visible which were not seen before. [*Of tinder.*]

Masters will eat their own possessions and their own workers. [*Of oxen which are eaten.*]

Men will come to be so ungrateful that they will load with blows the one who houses them without charge, to such an extent that much of his inside will be displaced and will go twisting about throughout the body. [*Of beating the bed to remake it.*]

Him who feeds them will be killed by them, and subjected to a pitiless death. [*Of things which are eaten, having first been killed.*]

The high walls of great cities will be seen upside down in their moats. [*Of the reflection of the walls of cities in the waters of their moats.*]

All the elements will be seen mixed together with a great disturbance, running now to the centre of the Earth, now to the sky, and at times rushing impetuously from the south to the cold north, sometimes from east to west, and similarly from this hemisphere to the other. [*Of water which in its course is muddy and mixed with earth, and of dust and cloud mixed with the air, and of fire with its heat mixed with all of them.*]

All men will of a sudden exchange the hemisphere. [*At any point a division can be made between the two hemispheres.*]

All creatures will move from east to west, and similarly from north to south. [*At any point there is a separation of east from west.*]

Bodies without soul will move of their own accord, and they will carry with them innumerable generations of the dead, taking riches away from those who live around. [*Of the movement of waters which carry timbers that are dead.*]

Oh, how many there will be whose birth will be forbidden! [*Of eggs which, once they are eaten, cannot become chicks.*]

Infinite generations will be lost with the death of those who are pregnant. [*Of fish which are eaten when they contain eggs.*]

Many of the masculine gender, through having their testicles removed, will be prohibited from procreating. [*Of animals which are castrated.*]

Milk will be taken from little children. [*Of the beasts which provide cheese.*]

Many Latin females will have their breasts cut off and taken together with their lives. [*Of* sommata² *made from sows.*]

Throughout Europe many peoples will mourn for the death of one man who died in the east. [*Of the mourning on Good Friday.*]

In the horns of animals sharp swords will be seen, by which many of their species will lose their lives. [*Of the handles of knives made from rams' horns.*]

The time will come when no difference will be seen between colours, all of them in fact being black. [*Of night, in which no colours can be distinguished.*]

He who by himself is gentle and harmless will become fearsome and fierce through bad company, and will very cruelly take the lives of many people – and he would kill even more if soulless bodies, issuing from caves, did not defend them. [*That is iron armour. Of swords and spears, which by themselves harm no one.*]

Many of the dead will rush to seize and bind the living, and they will keep them for their enemies to seek their death and destruction. [*Of snares and traps.*]

One will come from dark and gloomy caverns who will bring to the human race great troubles, dangers, and death. To many followers, after much trouble, he will give delight, and he who does not support him will die in poverty and disaster. He will be guilty of endless betrayals. He will increase the number of wicked men and induce them to be guilty of murder and robbery and enslavement. He will fill his supporters with misgivings. He will rob cities of their freedom, and men of their lives. He will cause trouble among men with many frauds, deceits, and betrayals. O monstrous being, how much better would it be for men if you were to go back to hell! Through him great forests will be stripped of their trees, and through him innumerable creatures will lose their lives. [*Of metals.*]

One will be born who, from a small beginning, will soon become great. He will have no respect for any created thing, but rather through his power almost everything will have the potential of being changed from one thing into another. [*Of fire.*]

Huge lifeless bodies will be seen to bear multitudes of men forcibly to the destruction of their lives. [*Of ships which sink.*]

Men of widely separated lands will be able to speak one with another and answer each other. [*Of writing letters from one country to another.*]

Men will speak to each other, and touch each other, and embrace each other, from one hemisphere to the other, and their languages will be understood. [*Of the hemispheres which are infinite and are divided by infinite lines in such a way that everyone always has one of those lines between his feet.*]

There will be many who, to practise their trade, will dress themselves in very rich clothes which they will seem to treat like aprons. [*Of priests saying Mass.*]

Wretched women will come of their own free will to reveal to men all their lustful and shameful and most secret actions. [*Of friars who hear confessions.*]

There will be many who will leave their duties and labours and their poverty of life and possessions, and will go to live in wealth and triumphant buildings, showing that this is the way to become a friend of God. [*Of the churches and dwellings of friars.*]

A very great multitude will sell publicly and tranquilly things of very great value, without a licence from the owner of those things, which were never theirs, and never in their power; and human justice makes no provision for this. [*Of Paradise for sale.*]

O human stupidity, o madness of the living! Simple people will bring many lights to light on their way all those who have completely lost the sense of sight. [*Of dead people who are being interred.*]

And where previously young women could not be defended against the lust and plunder of men, either by the custody of relatives, or by walled fortresses, the time will come when the fathers and relatives of these girls will have to pay a great price to those who wish to sleep with them, even if the girls are rich, noble, and very beautiful. This certainly makes it seem that Nature wishes to extinguish the human race, because it serves no useful purpose in the world and spoils all created things. [*Of girls' dowries.*]

Creatures will be seen upon the earth who will always fight amongst themselves, with very great harm, and even death, on all sides. There will be no end to their wickedness. Through their violent actions many trees from great forests of the world will be stricken down. And since they must be fed, their desire for nourishment will bring death and trouble and toil and fear and flight to all living beings. Through their boundless pride they will want to raise themselves to heaven, but the extreme weight of their limbs will keep them on the earth. There will be nothing on earth, or under earth or water, which will not be persecuted, removed, or ruined, or taken from its own land to another. And the bodies of these creatures will be a tomb and the way through which all the dead bodies of living beings must pass. O Earth, why do you not split open? And why do you not hurl into your huge gaping cavernous abysses, and hide from the light of the sky such cruel and merciless monsters? [*Of man's cruelty.*]

Trees from the great forests of Taurus and Sinai, the Appennines and Talas will be seen to glide through the air from east to west, from north to south, and take with them through the air a great multitude of men. Oh how many vows, oh how many dead people, oh how many separated friends and relations there will be, and how many who will not see their provinces again, or their homelands, and who will die without a tomb, with their bones scattered in various parts of the world! [*Of navigation.*]

Many will abandon their own dwellings, and take with them all their valuables, and will go to live in other districts. [*Of moving house on All Saints' Day.*]

And how many will mourn their ancient dead, bringing them lights! [*Of All Souls' Day.*]

Invisible coins will lead to the triumph of many who spend them. [*Of friars who, by spending words, receive great riches, and give Paradise.*]

Many will they be who by reason of ox-horns will die a grievous death. [*Of arches made from the horns of oxen.*]

I shall say a word or two or ten or more, as I wish, and I desire that more than a thousand people say the same thing at that time, that is, that they straightway say what I say, and do not see me, or hear what I say. [*This will be when you announce the time, and when you say a word, all those who like you are announcing the time, say the same number as you do at the same time.*]

Everything which in the winter is snowed under and hidden will be revealed and become manifest in the summer. [*Said of lies which cannot remain concealed.*]

What is it that is so much desired by men and, when it is possessed, cannot be known? [*It is sleep.*]

The leonine species will be seen breaking the earth open with its claws, and in the caves which it has made bury itself with the other animals which are subject to it.

Creatures clothed in shadows will come out of the ground and make astonishing attacks on the human race, which will be devoured by them with ferocious bites and shedding of blood.

Again: the foul flying creatures will glide through the air and attack even men and animals and feed on them with loud cries, and fill their own bellies with scarlet blood.

The blood will be seen coming out of the torn flesh and streaming down the surface of men's bodies.

Men will be seen suffering from such a cruel malady that they will scratch their own skin with their nails. [*That is scabies.*]

The plants and trees will be seen left without leaves and the rivers ceasing to run.

Seawater will rise above the high peaks of mountains towards the sky and will fall down again onto the dwellings of men. [*That is, by means of clouds.*]

The greatest trees of the forests will be seen carried by the fury of the winds from east to west. [*That is across the sea.*]

Men will throw away their own provisions. [*That is, by sowing.*]

The human race will come to such a pass that they will not be able to understand each other's language. [*That is a German with a Turk.*]

Fathers will be seen giving their daughters up to men's lust and rewarding these men and abandoning all their previous protection. [*When girls are married.*]

Men will issue from their graves in the shape of birds, and they will attack other men taking the food out of their hands and off their tables. [*Flies.*]

There will be many who will flay their mother and turn her skin inside out. [*Those who till the land.*]

Happy will they be who lend their ears to the words of the dead. [*Reading about their good works and noting them.*]

Feathers will lift men, as though they were birds, up into heaven. [*That is, by letters written with those feathers.*]

Things made by human beings will cause their deaths. [*Swords and spears.*]

Men will pursue what they fear the most. [*That is, they will live in poverty in order to avoid poverty.*]

Things that are separated will be reunited and have such power that they will restore lost memories to men. [*That is pages which are made of separate hides and hold the memory of the affairs and deeds of men.*]

The bones of the dead, in their rapid movement, will be seen to decide the fate of him who moves them. [*Dice.*]

With their horns oxen will prevent fire from dying. [*Lanterns.*]

Woods will give birth to children who will cause their death. [*Axe-handles.*]

Men will severely beat what gives them life. [*That is, they will thresh the grain.*]

The skins of animals will rouse men from their silence to loud cries and curses. [*Balls used in games.*]

Often the thing which is disunited will bring about great unity. [*That is the comb, made of separate teeth, which unites the threads in the cloth.*]

Wind passing through the skins of animals will make men jump. [*That is the bagpipes to which men dance.*]

Those who have done best will be beaten the most and their children taken away and flayed or rather undressed, and their bones broken and shattered. [*Of walnuts.*]

Alas! I see our Saviour crucified once more. [*Of sculptures.*]

Loud noises will issue from the graves of those who have died a nasty and violent death. [*Of men's mouths which are tombs.*]

The more one speaks with skins, which clothe feeling, the more wisdom one will acquire. [*Of the skins of animals which preserve the feeling which there is in the writings on them.*]

Almost all the tabernacles, in which the Body of the Lord is placed, will be clearly seen to go on their own account along different roads in the world. [*Of priests who have the Sacred Host inside them.*]

And those who feed grass will turn night into day. [*Tallow.*]

And many land and aquatic creatures will rise to the stars. [*The planets.*]

The dead will be seen carrying the living to various places. [*Carts and ships.*]

Many will have food taken out of their mouths. [*Ovens.*]

And those who are fed by others' hands will have the food taken out of their mouths. [*Of an oven.*]

I see Christ being sold and crucified once more and his saints martyred. [*Of crucifixes being sold.*]

Men will come to such a pass that they will be thankful that others triumph over their ills, that is over the real wealth they had lost. [*That is health. Doctors who live by illnesses.*]

Those who are dead will be the ones, after a thousand years, who will pay the expenses of many of the living. [*Of the religion of the friars who live by their saints, dead for a long time.*]

Many, who will be destroyed by fire, before this time will deprive many men of liberty. [*Of stones turned into mortar, with which prisons are built.*]

Many Francescos and Domenicos and Benedettas will consume that which on other occasions has been consumed by others nearby, and it will be many months before they can speak. [*Of infants at the breast.*]

Oh how many there will be who, when they are dead, will rot in their own houses, filling the surrounding atmosphere with a nasty stench. [*Of shells, and winkles which are rejected by the sea and rot inside their shells.*]

Wine is good, but water is better. [*On the table.*]

Of those, and they will be many, who entrust themselves to living near him, almost all will die a cruel death. Fathers and mothers, with their families, will be seen being devoured and killed by cruel animals. [*Of jackdaws and starlings.*]

Shadows will come east which will stain with darkness the sky above Italy. [*Of peasants who work in their shirtsleeves.*]

All men will flee to Africa. [*Of barbers*]

Very large figures in human shape will appear which, the closer they come to you, the more their great size will diminish. [*Of the shadow which a man makes at night with a lamp.*]

Many treasures and great riches will be near to four-legged animals, which will carry them to various destinations. [*Of mules which carry rich burdens of silver and gold.*]

He will be drowned who gives light for sacred rituals. [*Bees which make wax for candles.*]

The dead will come from below ground, and with violent movements they will drive innumerable human beings out of this world. [*Iron, which comes out of the ground, is a dead thing, and from it are made the arms which have killed so many men.*]

The highest mountains, although they are far from the sea-shores, will drive the sea out of its place. [*These are rivers which carry earth which they have removed from the mountains and unload it onto the seashores. Where the earth comes, the sea flees.*]

Water which has fallen from the clouds will change its nature in such a way that it will rest on the hillsides for a long time without moving. And this will happen in many different regions. [*Snowflakes, which are water.*]

The great stones of the mountains will emit fire which will burn the wood of many great forests and burn many wild and domestic beasts. [*Flint, which provides fire which consumes all loads of wood, by which forests are destroyed, and with which the flesh of animals is cooked.*]

Oh how many great buildings will be ruined by fire! [*By the fire from cannon.*]

Oxen will play a major part in bringing about the ruin of cities, and similarly horses and buffaloes. [*They pull the cannon.*]

Many will be those who grow as they fall. [*The snowball rolling on snow.*]

There will be a great crowd of those who, forgetful of their being and their names, will lie as though dead on the remains of other dead. [*Sleeping on birds' feathers.*]

The east will be seen to flow to the west, the south to the north, with the whole universe enveloped in a great din, fury, and tremor. [*The wind from the east which moves to the west.*]

The sun's rays will light fire in the earth by which what is beneath the sky will be lit, and being reflected they will go back down. [*The concave mirror lights the fire that heats the oven, which has its bottom beneath its top.*]

Much of the sea will fly up to heaven, and for a long time will not return. [*That is, in clouds.*]

Men will throw out of their own houses those victuals which were kept for preserving their lives. [*Of grain and other seeds.*]

Fathers and mothers will be seen to give much greater advantages to their stepchildren than to their true children. [*Of trees which nourish grafts.*]

Some will go with white vestments, moving arrogantly, and threatening with metal and fire him who has done no harm to them. [*Of censers and incense.*]

The times of Herod will return, because innocent children will be taken from their nurses and they will die with great wounds at the hands of cruel men. [*Of lambs.*]

Innumerable lives will be extinguished, and innumerable holes will be made over the earth. [*Of cutting grass.*]

Men will pass, once dead, through their own entrails. [*Of the life of men, whose flesh is changed every ten years.*]

Goats will take wine to the cities. [*Of wineskins.*]

Men will be glad to see their own works undone and broken. [*Cobblers.*]

How the prophecies can be divided. First things concerning rational creatures, second those concerning irrational creatures, third concerning plants, fourth ceremonies, fifth clothing, sixth circumstances or rather edicts or controversies, seventh circumstances which cannot occur in Nature, as for instance: 'the more you take away from that thing, the more it grows', placing the more important matters towards the end and the feeble ones at the beginning, and showing first the evils and then the punishments, eighth philosophical matters.

Prediction. Put in order the months and the ceremonies which are observed, and so make day and night.

Pleasantries

One man sees a big sword by the side of another man and says, 'O you poor thing! I see you have been bound to this weapon for a long time. Why don't you unbind yourself, since your hands are free and you are at liberty?'

To this the other replied, 'This is not something to do with you: in fact it's passé.'

The first man, feeling himself under attack, replied, 'I am so aware that you know little of the things of this world that I believed every well-known thing was new to you.'

While a certain man was arguing and boasting of knowing how to play many different practical jokes, one of those standing round said, 'I can play a joke by which I will get the breeches off anyone I want.' The first boaster, finding he was not wearing breeches, said, 'Oh no, you won't be able to get me to do it. Let's bet a pair of stockings.' The proposer of this game, accepting the challenge, borrowed several pairs of breeches and flung them in the face of him who had bet a pair of stockings. And he won the forfeit.

One said to an acquaintance of his, 'Your eyes have gone a strange colour.' He replied that this often happened to him. 'But have you done nothing about it? And when does this happen to you?' The other replied, 'Every time my eyes see your strange face, they find it so displeasing that they immediately turn pale and take on a strange colour.'

One said that the strangest things came to birth in his part of the world. The other replied, 'You, who were born there, confirm the truth of that by the strangeness of your ugly appearance.'

Two men were walking at night along a difficult way, and the one in front broke wind loudly. The other said, 'Now I see that you are fond of me.' 'How's that?' asked the first man. The other replied, 'You break wind so that I should know which way the wind blows and keep track of you.'

A woman was washing clothes and her feet were very red with cold. A priest who was passing by was amazed by this, and asked her where the redness came from. To this the woman replied straight away that she was standing on fire. Then the priest took in his hand that member which made him a priest rather than a nun and, drawing near to her, in a gentle and humble voice begged her to have the kindness to light that candle.

A priest was going through his parish on Holy Saturday and sprinkling the houses with holy water, as the custom is. He came to where a painter lived and, as he sprinkled the water on one of the paintings there, the painter, somewhat annoyed, turned round to him and asked why he was sprinkling the paintings. Then the priest said that it was the custom, that it was his duty to do so, and that he was doing the right thing, and that he who does the right thing can expect good and better things in return, and that this was what God had promised, and that for every good deed which one did on earth one would be rewarded a hundredfold from above. Then the painter, waiting until the priest had gone out, went to the window above and threw a large bucket of water over the priest, saying, 'Here is the hundredfold reward coming to you from above, just as you said would happen on account of the good deed which you performed for me with your holy water, ruining half my paintings.'

The Friars Minor observe fasting at certain times, during which they do not eat meat in their convents; but when they are travelling, because they have to live on alms, they are allowed to eat whatever is put in front of them. Now a couple of these brothers when they were travelling came to an inn in company with a certain rather shady merchant. When they were all together at the table which, because of the poverty of the inn, was provided with only one young cooked chicken, the merchant seeing that this was hardly enough for him alone, turned to the brothers and said, 'If I remember rightly, on such days as these you do not eat any kind of meat in your convents.' The brothers were forced by their holy rule to admit without any quibbling that this was true. And so the merchant had his wish. He ate the chicken, and the brothers made the best of things.

Now after this meal the companions, all three of them, went away together and, after they had travelled some way, they came to a wide and deep river. Since they were all on foot – the brothers because of their poverty, and the merchant because of his meanness – one of the brothers offered, in the way of fellowship, to go barefoot and carry the merchant across on his shoulders. So he gave him his sandals, and took the merchant on his back.

Then, when that brother was in the middle of the river, he remembered his holy rule once more. He halted, and like Saint Christopher, raised his head towards him who was weighing him down, and said, 'Please tell me. You haven't any money on you, have you?' 'Of course I have,' replied the merchant. 'How else do you think that we merchants carry on our business?' 'Alas,' said the brother, 'our holy rule forbids us to carry any money.' And with that he threw him into the water. The merchant, realising that the injury he had done had been wittily avenged, and almost blushing for shame, accepted the reprisal peacefully and with a friendly smile.

A man stopped having anything to do with a friend of his, because that man often spoke ill of his friends. The rejected friend one day complained to his former friend and begged him to give the reason why he had cast off their friendship. To this the other replied, 'I do not want to have anything to do with you any more because I like you and I do not want others to form a bad impression of you, as I have done, when you speak ill to them of me your friend. If we do not meet, it will seem that we are enemies, and when you speak ill of me, as you do, you will not be blamed for it so much as you would if we were still seen together.'

A man was trying to prove, on the strength of Pythagoras, that he had lived in this world previously, and another man would not let him conclude his argument. So the first man said, 'And as a sign that I have been here before, I recall that you were a miller.' The other, feeling that these words were an attack on him, confirmed the truth of that, saying that as a countersign he recalled that the first man had been the ass which carried the flour for him.

A painter was asked why, when he produced such beautiful figures, which were, after all, dead things, he produced such ugly sons. Then the painter replied that he made the paintings by day and the sons by night.

An old man was contemptuous of a young man in public, demonstrating boldly that he had no fear of him. And so the young man answered that his great age made a better shield for him than his tongue or his strength.

Just when a sick man was on the point of death he heard a knocking at the door. He asked one of his servants who was knocking, and the servant replied that it was someone who was called Lady Chastity. Then the sick man raised his arms to heaven, thanking God in a loud voice. And he told the servants to let her in immediately so that he might see a chaste lady before he died, since in his life he had never seen one.

When a man was told that he should get out of bed, since the sun was already up, he replied, 'If I had such a long journey to make and such things to do as he has, I would already have been up. However, since I have such a short distance to go, I shall not get up yet.'

A working man often came to visit a lord for no apparent reason, and the lord asked him what he was doing. He replied that he came there in order to have a pleasure which the lord could not have: he, like all ordinary people, was happy to see men more powerful than himself, while the lord could only see men less powerful than himself. Lords have to go without that pleasure.

A man reproached an honest man that he was illegitimate. The latter replied that he was a legitimate child of the human species according to natural law, and it was the other who was the bastard, because he behaved more like a beast than a man, and so couldn't be legitimate according to human laws.

Thoughts and Aphorisms

KNOWLEDGE AND EXPERIENCE

Of the soul. The movement of the Earth means that earth is pressed against earth, but the parts so struck move only a little. Water struck by water makes circles around the part which is struck. Even more so a voice sent into the air. More still when it is sent into fire. More also the mind when it goes out into the universe. But, since the mind is finite, it does not extend into the infinite.

We preserve our life with the death of others. In a dead thing insensate life remains which, when it is reunited with the stomachs of the living, regains sensitive and intellectual life.

Motion is the cause of all life.

Nature is full of infinite causes which have never been found out by experiment.

Knowledge is the captain, and practice is the soldiers.

Just as eating without wanting to is injurious to health, so study without the desire for it ruins the memory, and it retains nothing it has grasped.

Words which do not satisfy the ears of the hearer always cause boredom or displeasure. You will often see the signs of it when the hearers are full of yawns. And so, when you speak in front of men whose goodwill you desire, if you see such manifestations of displeasure, cut your speech short, or change the subject. If you do not do this, well then, instead of the desired thanks you will gain hatred and enmity.

And if you wish to see, without hearing him speak, what pleases someone, talk to him and change the subject several times. And when you see him gaze intently, without yawning or rolling his eyes or fidgeting, be certain that the subject of which you are speaking is the one which pleases him etc.

Of different branches of knowledge. There can be no certainty unless one can apply some branch of mathematics, or unless the subject is linked to mathematics.

O you who are of a speculative cast of mind, do not pride yourself on knowing things which Nature itself normally brings about. But congratulate yourself on seeing the result of those things which your mind has planned.

The error of those who rely on practice without knowledge. Those who are enamoured of practice without knowledge are like pilots who embark without a helm or compass, and never know for certain where they are going.

And many have set up shop with deceptions and feigned miracles, deceiving the foolish multitude, and if anyone shows that he understands their deceptions, they punish him.

Everyone wants to make some capital in order to give it to the doctors, the destroyers of life. And so they ought to be rich.

Experience, which is the interpreter between Nature the artificer and the human race, teaches us what Nature, constrained by necessity, works among mortals, which can only be brought about if the cause, her helmsman, teaches her how to operate.

There is no effect in Nature without a cause. Understand the cause, and you will have no need of experience.

Experience never fails. It is only our judgement which fails, as we promise ourselves a certain effect which is not brought about in our experiments. Because, given a principle, it is necessary that what follows is a true consequence of that principle, unless indeed there is some impediment. And even if some impediment is involved, the effect which should follow from the above-mentioned principle participates more or less in the said impediment, to the extent that this impediment is more or less powerful than the said principle.

Experience never fails. It is only our judgement which fails, seeking in our experience things which experience is not able to provide.

Men are wrong to complain of experience, which they strongly rebuke, accusing it of being deceptive. But we should leave experience alone, and turn our complaints against our own ignorance, which makes us leap ahead with our vain and foolish desires to promise ourselves something from experience which is not in its power to give, and then say that experience is deceptive.

Men are wrong to complain of poor innocent experience, accusing it of fallacious and lying demonstrations.

He who looks to experience for something which is not in its power to give, is being unreasonable.

How the eye, the rays of the sun, and the mind move faster than anything else. The sun, as soon as it appears in the east, immediately reaches to the west with its rays, which are composed of three spiritual qualities: splendour, heat, and the appearance of the power which has caused them.

The eye, as soon as it opens, sees all the stars of our hemisphere.

The mind leaps in an instant from east to west, and all other spiritual things move at a very different speed.

There is no blame in inserting into our arrangement of the process of knowledge some general rule which comes out of a preconceived conclusion.

Everything changes with time.

Given the cause, Nature brings about the effect in the shortest way possible.

No action done by Nature can be done more quickly with the same means.

Given the causes, Nature gives birth to the effects in the shortest ways possible.

Every instrument should be used with a knowledge of the experience from which it was born.

The question is raised whether all infinite things are equal or whether some are greater than others.

The response is that all infinite things are eternal, and eternal things are of equal continuance, but not of the same age, because that which was divided first has passed through longer ages, while the times to come are equal.

Just as every kingdom which is divided within itself cannot stand, so every mind which is distracted by various studies becomes confused and weakened.

The lover moves towards that which is loved, just as sense moves to what is sensible, and they are united and become one thing.
Work is the first thing which issues from the union.
If the thing loved is base, the lover becomes base.
When the thing which is united suits the uniter, delight and pleasure and satisfaction follow on.
When the lover is joined to the loved thing, he rests there.
When the weight is laid down, it rests there.
So with our intellect and the thing known by it.

There are four powers: memory and intellect, anger and concupiscence. The first two are reasonable and the others sensual.
   Of the five senses, sight and hearing and smell need little restraint, touch and taste need much.
   The sense of smell brings with it the sense of taste in dogs and other greedy beasts.

The more distant all the spiritual powers become from the first or second cause, the more space they occupy and the less relevant they become.

Every notion of ours originates from feeling.

Every man always finds himself in the middle of the world and beneath the middle of his hemisphere and above the centre of the world.

The senses are earthbound, and reason stands outside them when it contemplates.

The water you touch in a river is the last of what is going and the first of what is coming. So it is with present time.

Every action must be performed through movement.
To know and to wish are two human operations.
To discern, to judge, and to advise are human actions.
Our bodies are placed beneath the sky and the sky is placed beneath the spirit.

The soul can never be corrupted in the corruption of the body, but it acts like the wind which causes the sound of the organ so that, when one reed is broken, the wind cannot produce a good effect.

O investigators of perpetual motion, how many vain plans have you devised in such researches! You are in good company with those who try to transmute base metals into gold!

Nature seems to us here to have been a cruel stepmother rather than a mother to many creatures, and to others not a stepmother but a loving mother.

Every body is composed of those members and humours which are necessary for its maintenance. This necessity is well-known and provided for by the soul which has chosen this sort of body for its temporary dwelling.

Think of the fish which, because of the continual friction which there must be between it and water, is enabled by its soul, the daughter of Nature, to emit, through the porosity which there is where its scales join, a certain viscous liquid, which is hard to detach from the fish and which serves that purpose for the fish which pitch serves for a ship.

Necessity is the mother and teacher of Nature. Necessity is Nature's theme and its inventor, and it is the eternal restraint and rule.

Proverbs and Warnings

The memory of blessings received is feeble in the mind of the ungrateful.

Reprove a friend in private and praise him in public.

He who is afraid of dangers does not perish by them.

He who undermines a wall will find it falling on him.

He who cuts down a tree finds it is avenged in its fall.

Spare the traitor's life, because if he afterwards is loyal no one will trust him.

Ask for advice from him who knows how to correct himself.

Justice requires power, intelligence, and will, and it is comparable to the king of the bees.

He who does not punish evil is inviting it to be done.

If you seize a snake, its tail will bite you.

The ditch falls in on him who digs it.

He who does not restrain his appetites is one with the beasts.

One cannot have greater lordship, or lesser lordship, than over oneself.

He who thinks little errs often.

One can resist more easily at the beginning than at the end.

No advice is more trustworthy than that given from a ship in peril.

Expect trouble if you are guided by a young man's advice.

The void is born when hope dies.

Lust is the cause of generation.
Greed maintains life.
Fear or timidity prolongs life.
Pain is a preserver of the body.

Nothing is to be feared as much as notoriety. Notoriety is born out of vice.

Envy harms with its feigned infamy, that is by detraction, which is something that terrifies virtue.

Good repute flies up to the sky, because virtuous things are beloved of God. Ill-repute ought to be represented as upside down, because all its actions are contrary to the will of God and directed towards hell.

Golden ingots are refined in fire.

Every injury is unpleasant in recollection, except the greatest injury, death, which kills the recollection together with the life.

We do not ask for riches which can be lost. Virtue is our true good and the true reward for its possessor. It cannot be lost; it does not forsake us until life forsakes us. External goods and riches are always possessed along with fear, and often they leave their possessor to shame and mockery, when they are lost.

We do not lack ways and means of arranging and measuring off these wretched days of ours, and we should be glad not to spend them and pass through them in vain, without any praise, and without leaving any memory of ourselves in the minds of men. So that this wretched life should not be passed in vain.

The greatest happiness is the greatest cause of unhappiness, and the perfection of knowledge is the cause of stupidity.

Acquire in your youth what may refresh the infirmity of age. And if you intend your old age to be fed with knowledge, act while you are young in such a way that you may not lack for nourishment when you are old.

We do not judge things done at various times in the past at their right and proper distance, because many things which happened many years ago seem to be near to the present, and many recent events seem to be ancient, just like the antiquity of our youth. The eye does the same with things in the distance, which when they are illuminated by the sun seem close by to the eye, while many things which are close seem distant.

O you who are sleeping, what is sleep? Sleep is like death. Oh why do you not therefore perform such works that after death you will seem exactly like someone who is alive, rather than while you are alive resembling, in your sleep, the wretched dead?

Men and the animals are truly passages and conduits for food, the tombs of animals, the dwellings of the dead, giving life to themselves by the death of others, receptacles for corruption.

Just as animosity is a danger to life, so fear makes life safe.

Threats are the only weapons of the one who is not threatened.

When good fortune arrives, envy lays siege to it and fights, and when good fortune departs, it leaves behind it grief and repentance.

He seldom falls who walks well.

To give commands is lordly work; to work is a servile act.

He who is by nature foolish and wise by chance, when he speaks or acts naturally always appears foolish, and seems wise by chance.

A comparison with patience. Patience acts against injuries exactly as clothes act against the cold. Since if you put on more clothes as the cold grows greater, the cold cannot harm you. Similarly, if your patience increases as your injuries increase, these injuries will not be able to harm your mind.

Flying time glides by unnoticed and deceives us, and nothing is more rapid than the years, and whoever sows virtue reaps fame.

When I represented the Lord God as a child you put me in prison. Now, if I represent Him as an adult, you will treat me worse.

When I think I have learned to live, I shall learn to die.

He who wishes to see how the soul dwells in its body, should see how that body uses its everyday habitation. If that is without order and confused, then the body which the soul controls will be disordered and confused.

The methods of the swindler are the seeds of human blasphemies against the gods.

Mental passion drives lust away.

All creatures are languishing, filling the air with their laments, woods are crashing to the ground, mountains are opened for the plundering of the metals they generate. But what can I mention which is more wicked than people who praise to the skies those who have harmed their homeland and the human race most zealously?

Aristotle in the third book of his *Ethics*: men merit praise or shame only for those things which are in their power to do or not to do.

Just as iron when it is not used rusts, and water becomes stagnant or in the cold ices over, so the mind when it is not exercised rots.

The untamed cannot be constrained.

Cornelius Celsus.
The greatest good is wisdom, while the greatest ill is bodily pain. Since we are composed of two things, that is a soul and a body, of which the first is the better, and the body the worse, wisdom belongs to the better part, while the greatest ill belongs to the worse and worst part. The best thing in the mind is wisdom, as the worst thing in the body is pain. Therefore, just as the greatest ill is bodily pain, so wisdom is the highest good of the mind, of the wise man that is, and no other thing is to be compared to this.

Just as a day well spent brings happy sleep, so a life well employed brings a happy death.

The greater the feeling, the greater the suffering in pain.

Demetrius[3] used to say that there was no difference between the words and opinions of the inexperienced ignorant and the sounds and noises caused by a stomach full of wind.

And he had good reason to say this, because he did not think it mattered from what part they emitted the sound, whether from the lower part or from the mouth, because both had equal worth and substance.

Stupidity is the shield of shame just as importunity is the shield of poverty.

Pharisee means 'holy friar'.

A life well spent lasts long.

To speak well of a wicked man is the same as to speak ill of a good man.

And this man is completely mad. He is always struggling so that he might not struggle, and life passes him by while he lives in hope of enjoying what he has acquired with so much effort.

I obey you, my Lord, first because of the love which it is only reasonable I should have for you, and secondly because you can shorten or prolong men's lives.

Avoid those studies whose results die with the one who brought them about.

He is a bad disciple who does not go beyond his master.

There are those who should only be called conduits for food

and augmenters of excrement, because they put no virtue of their own into operation, and nothing remains of them but full privies.

Without doubt the truth is to lying as light is to darkness, and the truth is so excellent in itself that even when it refers to trivial and insignificant matters it far exceeds doubts and lies which concern great and elevated subjects. This is because our minds, even though they are accustomed to living among lies, cannot be satisfied with them, because the truth of things is the finest food for subtle intellects, but not for scatterbrains.

Lying is so contemptible that even if it said great things of God, it would lessen the attractiveness of His deity. And the truth is so excellent that, if it were to praise the meanest things, it would ennoble them.

But you who live in dreams prefer quibbling and deceptive arguments in things that are great and uncertain to those which are sure, natural, and not very elevated.

He who wishes to get rich in a day is hanged in a year.

Horace: 'God sells us all good things at the price of hard work.'

Truth was the only daughter of Time.

He who harms others does not make himself secure.

Fear is born sooner than anything else.

If you had a body worthy of your virtue you would be too big for this world.

You grow in reputation like bread in the hands of children.

Do not pledge yourself to do things and then not do them if you know that not having done them will distress you.

It does not seem to me that coarse men of bad habits and of little conversation deserve such a fine thing as the human body, or such a variety of machinery as do speculative men with much to discuss. They need only a bag to receive food and from which food may issue, and truly they cannot be considered as anything but a conduit for food, because it seems to me that they share no qualities of the human race but the voice and the shape, and in everything else they are less than beasts.

Flax is dedicated to death and the corruption of mortal beings: to death by snares and nets for birds, animals, and fish; to corruption by the linen cloths in which, when they are interred the dead, who decay in these cloths, are wound. And again, flax is not detached from its stalk until it begins to rot and decay. And it is what ought to be the crown and ornament in funeral rites.

Fables

The privet bush, feeling that his slender branches, covered with early fruit, were hurt by the wounding claws and beak of the troublesome blackbird, complained pitifully to the blackbird, and begged her, since she took his beloved fruit away from him, not to deprive him of his leaves, which protected him from the scorching rays of the sun, and not to flay him and strip him of his tender skin with her sharp talons. At this, the blackbird reproved him roughly: 'Be quiet, you uncultivated bit of scrub! Don't you realise that Nature has made you produce these berries for my nourishment? Can't you see that your purpose in the world is to provide me with such food? Don't you know, you bumpkin, that in the coming winter you will be food and nourishment for the fire?' The bush heard those words patiently and not without tears; but in a short time – when the blackbird had been caught in a snare and branches had been gathered to make a cage to keep her in – it happened that, among other branches, the slender branches of the privet were used for the bars of the cage. Then the privet, seeing that he was the means to deprive the blackbird of her liberty, rejoiced, and said, 'O blackbird, I am here and not yet consumed by fire, as you said I would be. I will see you prisoner before you see me burned up.'

When the laurel and the myrtle saw the pear tree being cut down, they cried out, 'O pear tree, where are you going? Where is all the pride you had when you were covered with ripe fruit? Now you will no longer shade us with your dense foliage.' Then the pear tree answered, 'I am going with the farmer who is cutting me down, and he will take me to the workshop of a fine sculptor, who with his art will give me the shape of Jove the god. I shall be dedicated in the temple, and adored by men as Jove, while you will often be maimed and stripped of your branches, which men will place upon me to honour me.'

A chestnut tree – seeing a man on top of a fig tree bending its branches towards himself and picking the ripe fruit from them and then putting it in his mouth and crushing it and destroying it with his hard teeth – shook its long branches and murmured in an agitated manner, 'O fig tree, you are less obliged to Nature than I am. You see how she has arranged for my dear children to be enclosed. First she has dressed them in soft shirts, on top of which she has put the hard skin with its lining, and – not content with such benefits – she has made a strong dwelling for them and over that has set a dense mass of sharp thorns, so that men's hands can do no harm.' Then the fig tree, together with her children, began to laugh, and when she had stopped laughing she said, 'You should know that men are so ingenious that, with rods and stones and twigs dragged among your branches, they can deprive you of your fruit. Then, when that has fallen, it is trodden underfoot and crushed with stones, so that your fruit comes out of its fortified dwellings torn and mangled. I, on the other hand, am touched carefully by the hand, and not beaten as you are with sticks and stones.'

The vain and wandering butterfly, not content with being able to fly easily through the air, and overcome by the delightful flame of the candle, resolved to fly into it. This joyful movement was the cause of a sudden sadness, because the light consumed the delicate wings. And the unhappy butterfly, lying scorched at the foot of the candlestick, after many tears and much regret, dried the tears from its swimming eyes, and lifting up its face said, 'O treacherous light, how often must you have beguiled me in the past. Oh, even if I did desire to see light, should I not have been able to distinguish the sun from your false lamp of filthy tallow?'

A walnut was carried by a crow onto a high bell-tower, and by falling into a crack in the wall was saved from the crow's deadly beak. The walnut begged the wall, by the grace which God had given it of being so great and eminent and enriched with such beautiful bells of such splendid sound, to come to its aid. It begged the wall not to abandon it, since it had not been able to drop under the green branches of its old father tree and lie on the fertile earth, covered with fallen leaves. After finding itself in the cruel beak of the cruel crow, and escaping from it by falling out, it wished to end its life in a little hole. The wall was moved with compassion at these words, and was happy to welcome the walnut into the place where it had fallen. And in a short time the walnut began to open, and take root in the cracks of the stones, and widen the cracks, and throw branches out from its cave. And the walnut, with its branches rising above the building and with its twisted roots growing bigger, soon started to break the wall open and to move the ancient stones out of their old places. Then too late and in vain the wall bewailed the reason for its harm, and, in short, it was broken open and much of it fell to ruin.

A monkey, finding a nest of little birds, approached it full of joy. But, since they were already able to fly, she could only take the smallest. She went back happily to her home with the bird in her hand. And, having examined this little bird, she began to kiss it, and in her excessive love she kissed it and brooded over it so much and grasped it so tightly that she took its life.

This has a message for those who, through not chastising their children, end up badly.

The poor willow tree, finding it could not have the pleasure of seeing its slender branches rise to their desired height and reach to the sky – it was always maimed and bare and spoilt because of the vines and whatever other plants grew nearby – gathered itself together and threw open the doors of its imagination. And it thought hard for a while, considering all the plants in the world, and wondering which one of them it could combine with that would not itself need any help or support. And after it had been engaged in such useful thoughts for a while, it suddenly thought of the pumpkin. Shaking its branches in great joy, it now thought that it had found the right companion in its need, because the pumpkin tends more to bind others than to be bound itself. Having made this decision, the willow lifted its branches to the sky, and waited for some friendly bird to act as a go-between in the matter. Then he saw a magpie nearby and he said to it, 'My dear bird, I beg you, by that haven which these days, in the mornings, you have found in my branches, when the hungry, cruel, and rapacious falcon wanted to eat you; and by that repose which I have often given you, when your wings required rest; and by those pleasures which you have enjoyed when you were entertaining your lovers among my branches – by all these I beg you to find a pumpkin and ask it for some of its seeds. Then say to those seeds, when they are born, that I shall treat them as well as if they had come from my own body. And use any other words which may be persuasive: since you are a master of language, I have no need to teach them to you.

And if you do this, I shall be glad to welcome your nest onto a fork among my boughs, together with your family, with no rent to pay.' Then the magpie, having agreed certain fresh terms with the willow – particularly that it would never welcome any snakes or beech-martens – raised its tail, lowered its head, and launched itself from the bough, trusting its weight to its wings. Beating its wings through the unresisting air, it looked here and there, steering itself by its tail. Eventually it found a pumpkin and, after some polite words of greeting, asked it for the seeds. The magpie brought them to the willow and was given a joyful welcome. Then with its feet it scratched the earth in a circle round the willow and with its beak planted the seeds there. In a short time the seeds grew and, as they grew and their branches spread out, they began to occupy all the spaces between the boughs of the willow and with their large leaves to hide from it the beauty of the sun and sky. And as if that were not enough, when the pumpkins arrived their unwonted weight dragged the tops of the tender branches to the ground, to their great torment and discomfort. Then the branches stirred and shook themselves in a vain attempt to make the pumpkins fall away from them, and they wasted several days in such fruitless efforts: their entanglement with each other frustrated such intentions. Then the willow, seeing the wind pass by, recommended itself to the wind, and the wind blew strongly. Then the old empty trunk of the willow split in two, right down to its roots, and it fell away into two parts. In vain it lamented its fate, and it realised that it had not been destined to have any good luck.

The flames had already lasted for a month in the glass-blower's furnace. When they saw a candle in a bright and shining candlestick placed near them, they were very anxious to approach it. One among them departed from its natural course and, drawing away from the wasted brand on which it had been feeding, and coming out of the furnace by a small crack, threw itself upon the candle which stood nearby and, with the utmost greed and voracity, devoured it almost completely. Then, wishing to prolong its own life, it tried to get back into the furnace which it had left. But this was in vain, and it was forced to waste away and die like the candle. Eventually, to its heartfelt regret, it turned into irksome smoke, leaving all its sisters to a long, beautiful, and splendid life.

Wine, the divine liquor of the grape, finding itself in a rich golden goblet and on Mohammed's table, and swollen-headed with so much honour and glory, was all at once struck by a contrary notion, and said to itself, 'What am I doing? Why am I pleased? Don't I realise that I am near to death, and about to leave the golden dwelling of the cup, and enter the ugly and stinking caverns of the human body, there to be transformed from a sweet-smelling and pleasing liquor into nasty, horrible urine? And as if that were not enough, to lie such a long time in ugly receptacles with other stinking and corrupt matter which has come out of the insides of human beings?' It cried to heaven, demanding vengeance for so much wrong, and begging that an end might be put at last to such contemptuous treatment. And it asked that, since that area produced the finest and best grapes in the whole world, at least they might not be turned into wine. Then Jove caused the wine which Mohammed had drunk to go to his head and make him mad, and this caused him to make so many mistakes that, when he came to himself again, he passed a law that no Asian should drink wine. And then the vines and their fruit were left alone.

A mouse was besieged in his little house by a weasel, which maintained a perpetual vigil in order to destroy him, and he could see his danger through a little hole. Meanwhile a cat came and straight away seized the weasel and ate it up. Then the mouse, having sacrificed some of his hazelnuts to Jove, gave thanks to the god for everything, and left his hole to repossess his former liberty, of which he was immediately, together with his life, deprived by the fierce claws and teeth of the cat.

When the spider found a bunch of grapes, which because of its sweetness was often visited by birds and different kinds of flies, it thought it had found a very convenient place for its deceitfulness. On its slender thread it went down into its new dwelling. Once there, it came every day to the spaces between the grapes and like a footpad it attacked the wretched creatures which were not on guard against it. And when several days had passed the harvester gathered the grapes, put them with others, and crushed them, and the spider with them. And so the grapes were a snare and delusion for the deceptive spider, as they were for the flies it deceived.

A small quantity of snow, finding itself stuck on top of a stone, which was itself placed on the peak of a very high mountain, began to use its imagination and said to itself, 'Now must I not be considered haughty and proud, being given such a high place, tiny scrap of snow that I am, and with such a great quantity of snow as I can see from here put much lower than I am? Certainly my small size is not worthy of this height, for I can easily see, and in my small self bear witness, what the sun did yesterday to my companions, who were in a few hours destroyed by the sun. And this happened to them through having been placed higher than they needed to be. I wish to flee from the sun's anger, and lower myself, and find a place suitable for my small size.' And it threw itself down and started to descend, and as it rolled from the high slopes onto more snow, the more it sought a low place, and the bigger it grew, so that, when it finished its descent down the hill, it found itself hardly smaller than the hill which held it up. And it was the last snow that summer to be dissolved by the sun.

This is about those who humble themselves and are exalted.

The falcon, not being able to bear the fact that the duck, as she flew from him, could go under water and hide, followed her under water. So his wings were soaked and he stayed in the water, while the duck rose in the air and mocked him as he drowned.

The fig tree, being near the elm and seeing the elm's boughs without fruit, and being anxious to have the sun on its own unripe figs, said to the elm reprovingly, 'O elm, aren't you ashamed to be in my way? Just wait until my children are grown up, and you will see what happens to you.' When those children were mature, a squad of soldiers happened to come along and, in gathering the figs, tore the tree and broke off its boughs. As the fig tree stood there, stripped of its limbs, the elm said, 'O fig tree, how much better it was to be without children than to get into such a wretched state because of them!'

What fire remained in a tiny piece of charcoal among the warm ashes was hungrily but inadequately feeding on the small amount of nourishment that was left. When the cook came into the kitchen to prepare the food as he always did, he put some wood on the fire which was almost dead, struck a match, and applied a light to the wood. Then he placed the cauldron above it and went away without any misgivings.

Then the fire, pleased with the dry wood that had been placed upon it, began to blaze up. Catching the air in the spaces between the pieces of wood, it wove its way through them in a cheerful and teasing way.

It started to breathe out through these spaces, which were like windows it had made for itself. And, sending out little shining and sparkling flames, it soon drove the dark shadows out of the crowded kitchen. And, together with the heat, the flames grew and played with the surrounding air, and their delightful murmurs sang with a sweet sound.

The fire, seeing that it had grown so strong and had risen so high above the wood, began to exchange its mildness and tranquillity for swollen and intolerable pride, and almost made itself believe that it could draw all of the superior element above the few pieces of wood.

And the flames, as they grew bigger and began to puff and pant and fill the whole fireplace with crackles and sparks, made their way towards the air, at which point the highest flames struck against the bottom of the cauldron above them.

The thrushes were delighted when they saw a man catch an owl and hold it prisoner by putting strong bonds on its feet. This owl was then, by means of birdlime, the reason why the thrushes lost, not their liberty, but their lives.

This is relevant to those countries which are happy to see larger countries lose their liberty, even though this means that they are without help from them and themselves remain in the power of their enemy, losing liberty and often life.

A dog was sleeping on the fleece of a ram. One of the dog's fleas, smelling the greasy wool, decided that it would be better to live there than feed on the dog, since there it would be safe from the dog's claws and teeth. Without thinking any more about it, it abandoned the dog and went in among the thick wool, and started to do its best to get through to the roots. After all its efforts it found that this attempt was in vain, because the wool was so thick that it was almost in one piece and there was no space through which the flea could get to the hide. So, after so much work and effort, it tried to return to the dog. But the dog had already gone away, and so the flea was constrained, after long repentance and bitter laments, to die of hunger.

A razor one day, coming out of that handle which is its sheath, and placing itself in the sun, saw the sun mirrored in its body. It gloried in this and, thinking it over, began to say to itself, 'Should I now go back to that shop which I have just come out of? By no means! Let it not please God that such splendour and beauty should be so abject! It would be madness if I were to perform such a mechanical operation as to shave the soapy beards of country yokels! Is this a body made for such work? Certainly not. I want to hide myself in some secret place, and there pass my life in rest and peace.' And so one day, after hiding for some months, it came out into the open again, and once it was out of its sheath, it saw that it had come to look like a rusty saw, and its surface no longer reflected the splendour of the sun. In vain repentance it lamented the irreparable harm, saying to itself, 'Oh how much better I was when I was with the barber and used my cutting edge which has now lost its sharpness! Where is my shining surface? This horrible tiresome rust has certainly destroyed it!'

The same thing happens to our minds when, instead of being exercised, they are given over to idleness. They then, like the razor, lose their cutting edge, and the rust of ignorance spoils their appearance.

A stone of some size, which had recently appeared above the surface of the water, was projecting in a place where there were grasses decorated with flowers of various colours, and where a delightful copse terminated at a stony road. The stone saw the great number of stones which were placed in the road below it, and felt the urge to let itself fall down there, saying to itself, 'What am I doing among these grasses? I want to live in the company of my sisters.' And it let itself roll and fall into the desired company. And it was soon in continual anguish from the wheels of carriages, the iron-shod feet of horses, and the feet of travellers. Some turned it over, some trampled on it, and at times, when it was a little raised, it was covered with mud and animal dung. It looked in vain at the place from which it had come, that place of solitary tranquillity.

This is what happens to those who wish to forsake the solitary and contemplative life and come to live in cities, among people who suffer endless adversity.

The painted butterfly, wandering about and speeding through the darkness, came across a lamp, and immediately went towards it. Circling round it again and again, it wondered at its splendour and beauty. Not being content merely to look at it, the butterfly went to it, as it was accustomed to do with sweet-scented flowers, and it directed its flight boldly to pass through the light, which consumed the ends of its wings and legs and other adornments. It fell to the foot of the lamp, and was full of wonder at what had happened to it, for it did not enter its mind that any evil or damage could come from such a beautiful thing. And, when it had recovered its strength a little, it took to flight once more and, passing through the light, was burned and fell straight away into the oil which fed the lamp. Enough life remained to it to allow it to consider the reason for its injuries, and it said to the lamp, 'O cursed lamp, I thought that I had found my happiness in you. Now in vain I regret my mad desire, and through my own harm I have come to recognise your destructive nature.' To this the lamp replied, 'This is how I treat those who do not know how to use me well.'

This is a symbol of those who, when confronted with lewd worldly pleasures, rush towards them like the butterfly, without considering their true nature, and who then, after long usage, come, in their shame and harm, to understand those pleasures.

The stone, feeling itself struck by flint, was astonished and said in a stern voice, 'How can you be so presumptuous as to trouble me? Stop upsetting me. You have given me a blow as though in revenge, and yet I have never annoyed anyone.' To this the flint replied, 'If you will be patient, you will see a marvellous result.' At this the stone calmed down and bore its sufferings with patience and fortitude, and saw itself give birth to a marvellous fire which was so powerful that it was useful for many things.

This is relevant to those who are fearful as they begin their studies, and then when they become able to control themselves and continue patiently with their studies, find that they achieve things that are marvellous to see.

Water, finding itself in the deep sea, its element, felt the urge to mount above the air and, helped by the element of fire, to rise in a thin vapour that seemed almost as thin as the air itself. And as it went higher it came to air that was thinner and colder, and there the fire abandoned it. And this water, being condensed into little grains, became heavy, and as it fell, its pride was turned into flight, and it fell right down from the sky. Then it was drunk by the dry earth where, imprisoned for a long time, it did penance for its sin.

The cedar, proud of its own beauty, scorned the trees around it. Once it had had them removed, the wind, with nothing to prevent it, uprooted the cedar and laid it upon the ground.

When the ant found a grain of millet, the grain, feeling itself seized by the ant, shouted, 'If you will do me the pleasure of letting me fulfil my desire to be born, I shall give you back a hundred for one.' And so it happened.

The clematis, being discontented in its hedge, started to cross the public road with its tendrils and cling to the hedge opposite. And so it was broken by travellers.

An ass, having fallen asleep on the ice of a deep lake, dissolved the ice with its own heat, and unfortunately only awakened when it was under the water, and immediately drowned.

The spider, which was hoping to catch the fly in its deceptive web, was, in its own web, cruelly put to death by the hornet.

The eagle, trying to make fun of the owl, found its own wings entangled and was taken by the man and killed.

The cedar wanted to produce a fine big fruit on its crest, and it put all its strength into achieving this. When the fruit had grown, it made the tall, straight tree bend down.

The peach tree envied the large quantity of fruit which it saw growing on the walnut tree, its neighbour. So it decided to do the same, and it loaded itself to such an extent that the weight of its fruit pulled it out of the ground by its roots and left it destroyed on the ground.

The walnut tree, showing above the road the riches of its fruit to all travellers, was stoned by them all.

When the fig tree was without fruit no one bothered with it. When it hoped to be praised by men after having fruited, it was bent by them and broken.

The spider, thinking it would have some peace in the keyhole, found death.

The lilac tree took root on the banks of the Ticino, and the current carried the river's bank away together with the lilac.

When the oyster was unloaded with other fish in the fisherman's house near the sea, it begged the rat to take it to the sea. The rat, intending to eat it, got it open and, as the rat was biting it, the oyster gripped its head and stopped it. The cat came and killed the rat.

The peasant, seeing the value of the vine, gave it many supports to hold it up, took the grapes and then pulled up the sticks and let the vine fall down, and burned its supports.

The crab waited under a stone to seize the fish which came there, and then the tide came with a ruinous rush of stones, and as they rolled along they shattered the crab.

The same thing:
The spider was waiting among the grapes to catch the flies which fed on them, and when the harvest came the spider was crushed together with the grapes.

The vine, which had grown old on the old tree, fell when the tree fell. It died together with the bad company it had kept.

The torrent bore so much earth and so many stones onto its bed that it had to change its course.

The net, which was used for catching fish, was taken and carried away by the fury of the fish.

The more the snowball rolled as it went down the snowy mountainside, the bigger it became.

The willow which, because of its long shoots, can grow to be bigger than any other tree, kept company with the vine, which is pruned every year, and as a result was itself always stunted.

Light is greedy fire above the candle.
Consuming that it consumes itself.

Wine consumed by a drunkard.
That wine avenges itself on its drinker.

Ink scorned for its blackness by the whiteness of the paper, which thinks itself sullied by it. The paper complained of being soiled by the blackness of the ink. The ink showed that the words which it composed upon the paper were the cause of the paper's conservation.

Fire, boiling water in a vessel, says that water does not deserve to be above fire, the king of elements, and so tries by the force of its boiling to drive the water out of the vessel. So the water, honouring the fire and obedient to it, goes down and puts the fire out.

The painter disputes and competes with Nature.

The knife, an artificial armament, deprives man of his nails which are a natural armament.

The mirror glories in holding the queen reflected in it and, once the queen has gone away, the mirror is left worthless.

By means of the file heavy iron is reduced to such thinness that a little breeze carries it away.

The plant complains of the old dry post that is put by its side and of the dry thorn-bushes which surround it. The one holds it upright, and the others keep it from bad company.

The pen needs to keep company with the penknife and useful friends like that, because one without the other is worthless.

Bestiary

Envy. We read that the red kite, when it sees that its little ones in the nest have grown too fat, out of envy pecks them in the side and keeps them without food.

Joy. Joy is characteristic of the cock, since it delights in every little thing and sings and frolics in all sorts of ways.

Sadness. Sadness is reminiscent of the crow. When it sees its newborn children are white, it goes away in distress and with great regret abandons them, and does not feed them until it sees that they have some black feathers.

Peace. We read that the beaver, when it is being hunted, knows that it is wanted for the sake of the medicinal value of its testicles, and so, when it can no longer flee, it stops and, in order to be left in peace by the hunters, it bites off its testicles with its sharp teeth and leaves them for its enemies.

Anger. They say that when a bear goes to a beehive to take away the honey, the bees start to sting so that it leaves the honey in order to take revenge. Then, since it wishes to be avenged on all those which have stung it, it gets its revenge on none of them, and its anger turns to rage, and it throws itself on the ground, and waves its paws and feet around, trying in vain to defend itself.

Gratitude. They say that the virtue of gratitude is seen best in those birds which are called magpies. Aware of the benefits of life and nourishment which they have received from their mothers and fathers, when they see them grown old they make nests for them and nurse them and feed them and with their beaks pull out their old and ugly feathers, and with certain herbs restore their appearance and well-being.

Cruelty. The basilisk is so cruel that, when it cannot kill animals with its venomous sight, it turns to herbs and plants and, fixing its gaze upon them, it dries them up.

Generosity. They say that the eagle is never so hungry that it does not leave part of its prey to those birds which are around it, and they, because they are not able to feed themselves, must pay court to the eagle in order to eat.

A lesson. When a wolf is moving cautiously round some building full of livestock and accidentally slips so that it makes a great noise, it bites its paw in order to teach itself to avoid such an error.

Madness. Since the wild ox hates the colour red, hunters cover a tree trunk in red, and the wild ox runs at it, and with the impetus its horns stick in the tree, and the hunters kill it.

Truth. Although partridges steal eggs from each other, the children born from those eggs always return to their true mother.

Fidelity or loyalty. Cranes are so faithful and loyal to their king that in the night, when he is asleep, some go round the meadow to watch from a distance, while others stay near to him. And each one holds a stone in her claws, so that if she were to be overcome by sleep, the stone would fall and make such a noise that they would all be roused. And there are others which sleep together around the king, and they do this every night, taking turn and turn about, so that they do not lose their king.

Duplicity. The fox, when it sees a flock of magpies or jackdaws or similar birds, at once throws itself on the ground in such a way, with its mouth open, that it seems to be dead. And the birds try to peck its tongue, and the fox seizes them by the head.

Lies. The mole has very tiny eyes and it always stays underground, and it lives for as long as it is hidden, and when it comes to light it immediately dies because it becomes known. So it is with lies.

Fortitude. The lion is never afraid, but fights boldly and fiercely against a multitude of hunters, always endeavouring to attack the first to attack him.

Fear or cowardice. The hare is always afraid, and the leaves which fall from the trees in autumn always frighten it and frequently put it to flight.

Magnanimity. The falcon only preys upon big birds, and it would sooner die than feed on little birds or stinking meat.

Vainglory. We read that the peacock is more subject to this vice than any other creature, because it is always contemplating the beauty of its own tail, spreading it in the shape of a wheel, and with its cry it attracts the attention of the other creatures around.

And this is the last vice to be overcome.

Constancy. The phoenix stands for constancy. When it wishes to be renewed, according to its nature, it is constant in its endurance of the burning flames which consume it, and then it is reborn once more.

Inconstancy. The swift stands for inconstancy. It is always in motion without experiencing the slightest discomfort.

Temperance. The camel is the most lustful creature there is, and it would travel a thousand miles after a female of the species, and yet when it is continually with its mother or sisters it never touches them, because it is so temperate.

Intemperance. The unicorn, through its intemperance and inability to control itself, and because of the delight which it has in maidens, forgets its ferocity and wildness. It lays aside all suspicion, goes to the seated maiden, and falls asleep in her lap. And so the hunters are able to seize it.

Humility. The best example of humility is the lamb. It submits to all other creatures, and when it is given as food to lions in a cage, it submits to them as to its own mother, so that it is often observed that the lions do not want to kill it.

Pride. The falcon, because of its hauteur and pride, wishes to lord it over and get the better of all the other birds of prey, and wishes that it may itself be the only one. It is often seen to attack the eagle, the king of birds.

Abstinence. The wild ass, when it goes to a spring to drink and finds the water muddy, is never so thirsty that it does not abstain from drinking or wait until the water is clear.

Gluttony. The vulture is so subject to gluttony that it would go a thousand miles to eat carrion and to follow armies.

Chastity. The turtle-dove is never false to its mate, and if one of them dies, the other observes perpetual chastity, and never rests upon a green bough and never drinks pure water.

Moderation. The ermine or stoat, in its moderation, eats only once a day, and would sooner let itself be caught by hunters than take refuge in a filthy den. This is in order not to sully its nobility.

The eagle. The eagle, when it is old, flies so high that it scorches its feathers, and Nature allows it to renew its youth by falling into a little water. And if its young cannot endure the sight of the sun, it does not feed them. No bird which does not wish to die approaches its nest. All creatures fear it greatly, but it does not harm them. It always leaves them the remains of its prey.

The pelican. This creature has a great love for its young, and when it finds them dead in the nest from a serpent's bite, it reacts by piercing its own breast and, bathing them in showers of blood, it brings them back to life.

The salamander. The salamander's limbs are not sensitive, and it likes no food but fire, and often it renews its skin in fire.

The chameleon. This creature lives on air. But in the air it is open to attack from the birds, so to be safe it flies above the clouds, and there it finds air that is so thin that it cannot sustain any bird which might follow it.

No one goes to this height, where the chameleon flies, unless heaven permits it.

The ostrich. This creature converts iron – which nourishes soldiers once it is converted into arms – into food. It hatches its eggs by looking at them.

The swan. This creature is pure white, without any spot, and it sings sweetly as it dies, and with that song it ends its life.

The stork. This creature drives evil away from itself by drinking salt water. If it finds its mate is unfaithful it forsakes it. And when it is old, its young nurse it and feed it until it dies.

The cicada. The song of this creature silences the cuckoo. It dies in olive oil, and revives in vinegar. It sings in blazing heat.

The bat. This creature is blinder where there is most light, and the more it looks at the sun the blinder it becomes.
    This is like vice, which cannot exist where there is virtue.

The asp. This creature carries sudden death in its teeth and, so as not to hear spells, it stops its ears with its tail.

The dragon. This creature binds the elephant's legs so that the latter falls upon it and they both die. It gets its revenge by dying.

The viper. This creature opens her mouth during coitus, and at the end she clenches her teeth and kills her mate. Then, when the children have grown inside her, they tear her womb open and kill their mother.

The scorpion. If, on an empty stomach, you spit saliva onto a scorpion, you will kill it.

This is reminiscent of abstinence from greed, which removes and destroys the illnesses caused by that greed and opens the way to virtue.

The crocodile: hypocrisy. This creature seizes a man and kills him straight away. When it has killed him, it mourns and laments for him with many tears, and when it has finished its lament, it devours him mercilessly.

This is what the hypocrite does whose eyes fill with tears at the slightest thing, while he has a tiger's heart, and rejoices inwardly at other people's misfortune with a face full of pity.

The caterpillar: of virtue in general. The caterpillar, which zealously and skilfully has woven about itself a new dwelling with remarkable artifice and subtle endeavour, issues from it with beautiful colourful wings, and with them it goes up to the sky.

The tarantula. The bite of the tarantula keeps a man to his first resolution, that is, what he was thinking of when he was bitten.

The elephant. The great elephants have in their nature what is seldom found in men. That is honesty, prudence, and fairness, and religious observance. We know this because when the moon is new, they go to rivers, and there they wash and solemnly purify themselves, and having greeted the moon they return to the woods. And when they are ill they lie on their backs and throw grass towards the sky, almost as if they wished to offer sacrifice. When old age makes their tusks fall out, they bury them. Of their two tusks, they use one to dig up roots to feed upon, and they keep the other sharp for fighting. When they are overtaken by hunters and overcome by weariness, they knock their tusks out, and with them they buy their freedom. They are merciful, and they are aware of danger. And if they find a man alone and lost, they are glad to put him back on the right track. If one of them finds the footprints of a man before it sees the man himself, it fears a trap, and so it stops and snorts, and shows the footprints to the other elephants, and they band together and go cautiously. They always go in herds, with the oldest in front, and then each according to age, and so the herd is organised. They have a great sense of shame, and they only have intercourse at night and in hiding. And after intercourse they do not return to the herd until they have washed in a river. They do not fight over females as other creatures do, and they are by nature so merciful that they are unwilling to harm those weaker than themselves. If they come across a herd of sheep, they guide them to one side with their trunks so as not to crush them underfoot, and they never do any harm if they are not provoked.

When one falls into a ditch, the others fill the ditch up with boughs, earth, and stones. In this way they raise the bottom of the ditch, and the captive is easily freed. They are very afraid of the squealing of pigs, but even as they run away they do not do any harm at all with their feet, except to their enemies. They like rivers and are always wandering about near them, but because of their great weight they cannot swim. They devour stones, and tree-trunks are to them delightful food. They hate rats. Flies like their smell and settle on their backs, and the elephants tear their own skin and drive the flies into the narrow folds of the skin and kill them. When they cross rivers they send their young downstream, and they place themselves upstream and break the force of the water so that its current does not wash their young away.

The dragon throws itself under the elephant's body, ties its legs with its tail, and with its wings and claws binds the elephant's sides, trying to slaughter it with its fangs. And then the elephant falls onto the dragon, which is crushed to death. And so with the death of its enemy the elephant is avenged.

Serpents. The serpent, which is a very large creature, when it sees a bird in the sky, inhales so forcefully that it draws the bird into its mouth. Marcus Regulus, a consul in the Roman army, was with his army attacked by some such creature and almost destroyed. When this creature was killed by a siege engine, it measured 125 feet. With its head, it was taller than any tree.

Lions, leopards, panthers, tigers. These beasts keep their claws sheathed, and they do not unsheathe them except when they are upon their prey or an enemy.

The lioness. When the lioness defends her young against hunters, she lowers her eyes to the ground so as not to be frightened by the spears. This is because if she took to flight her young would be captured.

The lion. This terrible animal fears nothing so much as the noise of empty carts and also cocks crowing. It is very frightened when it sees a cock, and looks at its comb in terror, and even when it has its face covered loses all heart.

The African panther. This animal is shaped like a lioness, but its legs are longer and its body longer and slimmer. It is completely white, except that it is dotted with black spots like rosettes. All the other animals are delighted to see it, and they would always be standing round it if it were not for the terror inspired by its face. Knowing this, it hides its face, and the animals around feel secure and come closer in order to enjoy its beauty more, and then the panther suddenly snatches the nearest one and straight away devours it.

Camels. The Bactrian camels have two humps, the Arabian camels one. They are swift in battle, and very useful as beasts of burden. This animal observes strict rules and regulations: it refuses to move if it has a greater load than usual, and similarly, if it has to travel too far, it stops suddenly and the merchants have to put up for the night.

The cerastes. This creature has four little movable horns. When it wishes to eat, it hides itself in foliage, except for its horns which, as they move, seem to the birds to be little frolicking worms. Then the birds swoop down to peck them, and the cerastes suddenly wraps itself round the birds and devours them.

The amphisboena. This has two heads, one in the usual place, and the other in its tail, as if it were not enough to spit venom from one place only.

The asp. The only remedy for a bite from this animal is to cut away the affected part immediately. This pernicious animal has such affection for its mate that they always go together. If one of them has the misfortune to be killed, the other follows its killer at an incredible speed, and it is so diligent and prompt in its revenge that it overcomes every difficulty. It passes through whole armies, seeking to harm only its enemy, and covers great distances, and it can only be avoided by going through water or fleeing very rapidly. Its eyes are turned inward and it has large ears, so it is more affected by sound than by sight.

The ichneumon. This animal is born in Egypt. It is the mortal enemy of the asp. When it sees an asp nearby, it rushes to the Nile's mud and covers itself with it, and when it has dried in the sun, it smears itself with mud again, and so by drying one coat of mud after another it has three or four garments like armour, and then it attacks the asp and, seizing the right moment, it catches it in its throat and drowns it.

The crocodile. This is born in the Nile, has four feet, is dangerous on dry ground and in the water, is the only land animal without a tongue, and it bites by moving only its upper jaw. It grows to a length of forty feet, has claws, and is armed with a leathery hide which can withstand any blow. It spends the day on land and the night in the water. When it has fed on fish, it goes to sleep on the banks of the Nile with its jaws open, and the bird known as the trochilus, a very tiny bird, runs to its mouth and jumps about and pecks away the food that remains in the front and back teeth, giving the crocodile so much pleasure by tickling it that it makes the crocodile open its jaws wider and sleep more profoundly. When the ichneumon sees this, it dashes into its mouth, and pierces its stomach and entrails, and ultimately kills it.

The ibis. This is like a stork. And when it feels ill it fills its throat with water and with its beak makes an enema.

The weasel. When it goes hunting rats, this animal first eats rue.

The boar. This animal treats its ailments by eating ivy.

The snake. When it wishes to be renewed, this creature casts off its old skin, starting with the head. It takes a day and a night to change.

The chameleon. This always takes on the colour of its background, with the result that it is eaten by the elephant together with the foliage against which it is standing.

Foresight. The cock does not crow until it has flapped its wings three times. The parrot, when it goes from bough to bough, never places its foot where it has not first placed its beak.

Fantastic Descriptions

To the Representative
of the Holy Sultan of Babylon

I shall tell you everything, point by point and in order,
showing first the effect and then the cause of the recent
disaster which occurred in these northern parts of ours, and
which I am certain must strike with terror not only you, but all
the universe.

Finding myself in these parts of Erminia and about to
perform lovingly and carefully that duty with which you have
charged me, I went into the city of Calindra, which is close to
our borders. This city is situated on the slopes of that side of
Mount Taurus which is divided from us by the River
Euphrates, and it faces the peaks of great Mount Taurus to the
west. These peaks are so lofty that they seem to touch the sky,
for there is no earthly part of the universe higher than the
summit of this mountain, which the sun's rays in the east
always strike four hours before daytime. And, because it is of
pure white stone, it shines out to the inhabitants of Erminia
like bright moonlight in the dark. And it is so high that it rises
four miles vertically above the highest clouds. From much of
the west this summit can be seen lit up by the setting sun up to
a third of the way through the night. This is what, when we
were with you in clear weather, we judged to be a comet,
apparently changing its shape several times in the darkness
of the night, sometimes dividing itself into two or three, and
sometimes growing long and sometimes shortening. This
appearance is caused by the clouds which on the sky's horizon
interpose themselves between part of this mountain and the

sun. With the sun's rays cut off, the light from the mountain is interrupted by clouds of various lengths, and hence the variations in its shape and splendour.

I should not be accused by you of laziness, as your reproofs would seem to suggest. It is rather that your boundless love, to which I owe the benefits I have received, has constrained me to seek out with the utmost care and investigate with diligence the cause of such a great and astounding effect; and this is something which I have not been able to do without taking some time over it. Now, in order to satisfy you as to the cause of such a great effect, I must indicate to you the nature of the site, and then I will arrive at the effect, with which, I believe, you will be well satisfied.

Do not complain of my delay in replying to your welcome request, because these things which you ask me about are natural things which cannot be explained in an instant. This is particularly the case because, in order to reveal the cause of such a great effect, it is necessary to describe the site according to the correct procedure. By this means you will be easily able to satisfy your curiosity.

I shall omit a description of the shape of Asia Minor and of the lands and seas which enclose it, because I know that your industrious and careful studies have not kept you ignorant of such matters. Instead, I shall outline the true shape of Mount Taurus, which is the cause of such a stupendous and disastrous marvel, and this will serve our purpose.

This Mount Taurus is said by many people to be the range of Mount Caucasus. However, wishing to be clear in my mind about it, I have spoken with some of those who live by the Caspian Sea, and they point out that, although their mountains have the same name, they are higher, and this confirms that Mount Taurus is the true Mount Caucasus, because in the Scythian language 'caucasus' means 'the greatest height'. And indeed there are no reports of such a high mountain either in the east or in the west. And the proof that this is so is that the inhabitants of the lands to the west see the rays of the sun lighting up part of its peak for a quarter of the longest night, and a similar thing occurs in those lands which lie to the east.

The Taurus Range throws a huge shadow which, when the sun is at its meridian in the middle of June, extends as far as the border with Sarmatia which is twelve days' journey away, and in the middle of December extends to the Hyperborean Mountains, which are a month's journey to the north. And the lee side of the mountain is always full of cloud and mist, because the wind, which breaks in two as it strikes the rock, closes up again afterwards and so brings together clouds from all sides and leaves them to strike against each other. And the lee side is always afflicted by thunderbolts, owing to the multitude of clouds which come together there, so that the rock there is broken up into great pieces.

The land round the base of this summit is inhabited by people who are very rich, and there are many fine springs and rivers, and the land is fertile and produces abundant crops of many kinds, particularly in those parts which face south. However, when one climbs about three miles, one starts to find woods of great fir trees, pines, and beeches, and similar trees. Then another three miles after this there are meadows and wide stretches of pasture. All the rest, right to where Mount Taurus begins, is always covered with snow, which never leaves it and which extends to the height of about fourteen miles in all. From where the mountain begins up to the height of one mile, there are never any clouds. The track winds for fifteen miles up to the summit, which is at a height of about five miles vertically. And so we come to the peaks of Taurus where, from halfway up, we begin to feel warm air and there is no breath of wind, but where nothing can grow very well. Nothing lives here but some birds of prey, which nest in the high fissures of Taurus and descend below the clouds to seize their prey on the grassy slopes. Here – that is, above the region of clouds – there is nothing but rock, rock of a dazzling whiteness. The summit itself is inaccessible, since the ascent is rugged and dangerous.

Having written to you several times to congratulate you on your good fortune, I know that now, as a friend, I shall make you sad for my sake, because of the wretched state in which I find myself. The fact is that recently I and these wretched country-folk have been in such distress, fear, danger, and harm, that we have been longing for death. And I really could not believe, since that far-off time when the elements did away with aboriginal Chaos by separating one from another, that they would reunite, in all their strength and indeed anger, to do so much harm to men as now we have both seen and experienced. This disaster is such that I do not imagine anything could make it worse. To begin with we were attacked and assaulted by the force and fury of the winds. To this was added the fall of great mountains of snow which filled up all these valleys and shattered much of our city. Then fortune, not content with this, submerged all the lower part of this city with sudden floods of water. On top of this there was a sudden rainfall – or rather a stormy precipitation full of water, sand, mud, and stones – all mixed up with roots, twigs, and the stumps of various trees, and everything rushing through the air and falling on us. Last, a blazing fire, which seemed to be borne not on the wind but by thirty thousand devils, has scorched and devastated all this land, and still has not stopped. And those few of us who have survived, have survived in such dismay and fear that, like dolts, we have hardly dared to speak to each other. Having abandoned all our usual occupations, we have come together in certain ruined churches, men and women, and children and adults, all mixed together like herds of goats. And if it were not that certain peoples have come to our aid with provisions, we should all be dead from hunger.

Now you see what a state we are in. And all these misfortunes are nothing in comparison with what we can expect very soon.

I know that, as a friend, you will be saddened by my misfortunes, just as I, in my letters, have shown how pleased I was at your good fortune.

Out of pity our neighbours have come to our aid with provisions, although they used to be our enemies.

THE GIANT

Dear Benedetto Dei,[4]

The news here in the east is that in the month of June a giant has appeared, coming from the Libyan desert.

This giant was born on Mount Atlas, and was black, and had Artaxerxes against him, together with the Egyptians and the Arabs, the Medes and the Persians. He lived in the sea where are found whales, sperm whales, and ships.

When this fierce giant fell, on account of the land being muddy and drenched in blood, the countryside looked as though it had suffered an earthquake, and there was great fear of Pluto, the god of the underworld. And because of the great blow, he lay on the flat earth more or less stunned. So then the people, thinking that he had been killed by a thunderbolt, returned in a great crowd. Like ants which rush across the trunk of a fallen oak, they streamed over his huge limbs, often wounding him as they went.

The giant, feeling himself almost completely covered with this multitude, and being tormented by their stings, gave a bellow which sounded like fearful thunder. Then, placing his hands on the ground and raising his frightening face, and putting one of his hands on his head, he found that it was covered with men, who were hanging onto his hair, like those tiny creatures which are born there. So he shook his head, and the people fell off through the air like hail when it is driven by the fury of the winds. And many of these people were found to be dead by those who showered down on top of them and then trod them underfoot.

And holding onto his hair, and contriving to hide amongst it, they were like sailors in a storm who run amongst the ropes to lower the sails and thus avoid the full force of the wind.

Mars, fearing for his life, took refuge beneath Jove's bed.

For a start, the black visage is very horrible and frightening to look at, and particularly the red sunken eyes under the fearful black brows, which are fit to make the weather cloudy and make the earth tremble.

And, believe me, there is no man so brave that he would not immediately take to flight, if this giant's inflamed eyes were turned upon him, for hellish Lucifer's face would look like the face of an angel in comparison with this: the wrinkled nose with its flaring nostrils from which issued huge tufts of bristles, the twisted mouth beneath with its thick lips at whose extremities were whiskers like those of a cat, and the yellow teeth. The instep of his foot is higher than the head of a man on horseback.

His anger turned to fury, which induced him to go into the crowd, and kick the people up into the air, so that they fell down on each other like a dense storm of hail. And this savagery continued until the dust, which his huge feet had kicked up into the air, forced this hellish fury to fall back.

And we continued to flee.

Oh how many different assaults were made upon this infuriated creature to whom all attacks were as nothing! O wretched people, your indestructible fortresses are of no avail, and the high walls of your cities, and your great multitude, and your houses and palaces! There is nothing left for you but tiny holes and subterranean caverns. You are looking for refuge or trying to escape like crabs or crickets or similar creatures!

Oh how many unhappy mothers and fathers lost their little children! Oh how many wretched women were deprived of their friends!

Truly, truly, my dear Benedetto, I do not believe that there was ever seen, since the creation of the world, such public lament and so much terror!

Certainly in situations like this the human race has reason to envy every other species. If the eagle is more powerful than all other birds, the smallest birds remain unvanquished because of their speed: the swallow is nimble enough to escape from the merlin; the dolphin flees so fast that it escapes from the whale – even the sperm whale. But we alone, alas, find no safety in flight, since this giant, even when he is walking slowly, goes very much faster than any racehorse. I do not know what to say or do. I seem to see myself plunging head down into the great throat, to end up huddled in death and buried in his great belly.

The powerful branching fins with which, as you pursued your prey, you ploughed the salt waves, stormily breasting them and opening them up before you, availed you nothing.

Oh, how often were shoals of dolphins and great tuna seen fleeing in terror before your cruel fury! And you, striking with your swift and spreading fins and your forked tail, caused a sudden tempest in the sea with a great thunder and sinking of ships. And with the great waves you caused, you covered the open shores with terrified and bewildered fish. Fleeing from you and thrown up on dry land, they became the super-abundant prey of the people thereabouts.

O Time, swift predator on all created things, how many kings, how many peoples have you destroyed, and how many changes of fortune and varied accidents have you brought about, since this marvellously formed sea beast died here!

Oh how often were you seen in the waves of the mighty swollen ocean, overcoming and standing out above those waves like a mountain, and with your dark bristly back ploughing the waters of the sea, in superb and solemn motion!

Fragments of a Spiritual Autobiography

There is not such a bellow from the stormy sea, when the north wind strikes it, in the foamy waves between Scylla and Charybdis; nor from Stromboli or Mongibello when their sulphureous flames break out of the great mountains in which they are enclosed and, as they are vomited out, shoot rocks and earth into the air; nor when the red-hot caverns of Mongibello restore the element they could not retain, spewing it up and violently thrusting it back into its proper place, driving before it any obstacle that stands in the way of its impetuous fury.

And drawn by my avid desire to see the great abundance of varied and strange shapes assumed by Nature's ingenuity, roaming a little among shadowy crags and stumbling-blocks, I came to the entrance of a great cave. I paused a while in front of it in astonishment and ignorance. Then I bent down, placed my left hand on my knee, and with my right hand shaded my lowered half-closed eyes. I kept bending forwards here and there to see if I could make out anything inside; but this was impossible because of the great obscurity within. After a short while I suddenly experienced two feelings: fear and desire – fear of the dark and threatening den, and desire to see if there was any extraordinary thing inside it.

Those men are pompous and swollen with pride, clothed and adorned in other men's labours, not their own. They do not acknowledge my achievements even to my face. Now, if they despise me as a discoverer, how much more are they to be despised, who are not discoverers, but merely the trumpeters and reciters of other men's works.

Men who are discoverers and interpreters of Nature to other men should be judged and valued – in comparison with the reciters and trumpeters of other men's works – exactly like the object in front of the mirror in comparison with this object as it appears in the mirror: the one is something, and the other is nothing. The latter are people who are poorly endowed by Nature, and possess only those abilities which they have acquired by study and effort, without which I would place them among the beasts of the field.

Many will think that they are right to find fault with me, declaring that my proofs go against the authority of some men who are (according to their inexpert judgement) much to be respected, not realising that my ideas are simply the result of experience – the true teacher.

Realising that I cannot deal with matters of very great use or delight, since those who were born before me have taken all useful and essential themes for their own, I shall do as he does who by reason of his poverty arrives last at the fair, and not being able to provide himself with anything else, takes all those things which others have already seen and not accepted but rejected as of little value. I shall take this despised and rejected merchandise, passed over by many buyers, and place it upon my own back, and I shall go and distribute it, not in great cities, but in poor villages, accepting such reward as what I have given may deserve.

All good men naturally have a desire for knowledge. I know that many will say that this is a pointless exercise. And they will be those of whom Demetrius remarked that they regarded the wind which formed words in their mouths as of no more account than the wind which issued from lower down in their bodies. Such men desire only bodily riches and pleasure, and are quite without the desire for knowledge, which is true wealth and food for the soul, because, just as the soul is worth more than the body, so are the riches of the soul worth more than those of the body. And often when I see one of them take a work in hand, I wonder whether, like a monkey, he will put it to his nose, or whether he will ask me if it is something to eat.

I know well that, because I am not a literary man, some presumptuous people will think they are right to upbraid me by saying that I am unlettered. Stupid people! They do not realise that I could reply as Marius[5] did to the Roman patricians, 'Those who adorn themselves with other people's achievements do not wish to make open acknowledgement of mine.' They will say that, because I am unlettered, I cannot express properly what I want to say. They do not know that my ideas are drawn from experience rather than from other people's words. Experience was the teacher of those who have written well, and so I take it for my teacher and bring it to bear on all things.

Now look, reader, at what our ancestors would have us believe. They tried to define life and the soul, dealing with things which cannot be proved, when those things which at all times could be clearly known and proved by experience have been unknown for so many centuries or else misunderstood. The eye itself, which exists so clearly for the purpose of gaining experience, has right up to my times been defined by an infinite number of authors in one way, and I find by experience that it is something quite different.

The effect of my rules. If you said to me, 'What effect do your rules produce? What good are they?' I should reply that they restrain engineers and researchers from promising to themselves or others things which are impossible, a procedure which would lead to their being thought mad or fraudulent.

The definition of the soul I leave to the intellects of the religious brothers, fathers of the people, who through inspiration know all secrets.

I do not meddle with royal decrees, because they are the perfection of truth.

He who in disputes brings authority to bear is not using his mind but his memory.

Good writings are born out of a natural talent, and since we should praise the cause more than the effect, you will praise a natural unlettered talent more than a capable literary man without natural talent.

There are so many words in my native language that I complain rather of not understanding things well than of a lack of words with which to express properly the ideas in my mind.

O writer, what words of yours can provide such a perfect representation as a drawing does? In your ignorance you write confusedly and leave little understanding of the true shape of things when you have to speak of the representation of something corporeal on a flat surface, although you deceive yourself into believing you can fully satisfy your hearer. But I suggest that you do not trouble yourself with words except when speaking to blind people. And even when you do wish to appeal with words to the ears and not the eyes of men, speak of the essence of things, and do not concern yourself with visual matters and with trying to convey them through the ears, because you will be easily outdone by the works of painters.

How can you describe this heart without composing a whole book on the subject? And the more you write at length and in detail, the more you will confuse the hearer's mind. And you will need commentators, or you will need to go back to experience, of which you have very little, and which informs you of very few things regarding this whole subject, which you really want to know all about.

O investigator of this anatomy of ours, do not be saddened by the fact that your knowledge is bought with someone else's death, but rejoice that our Creator has concentrated your mind on such an excellent instrument.

And you, man, who can see in these labours of mine how wonderfully Nature works, if you consider it a wicked thing to destroy what Nature makes, judge how infamous it is to take away a man's life, considering his marvellously constructed body, which is nothing in comparison with the soul which dwells within. Truly, whatever the soul may be, it is something divine, and so you should let it live in its home as long as it wishes, and not allow your anger or malignity to destroy such a life. I really do not know what punishment he deserves who does not respect the soul. For the soul is very unwilling to leave the body, and I really believe that its lamenting and grief are not without cause.

And try to stay healthy, which you will manage to do more successfully the more you keep away from doctors, whose prescriptions are a kind of alchemy, of which there are as many books as there are of medicine.

1. A thin plate of translucent horn was at one time used instead of glass in lanterns.

2. *Sommata* is a dish made from salted pork loin.

3. A Cynic philosopher in Rome in the first century AD.

4. A merchant, an acquaintance of Leonardo, who had travelled much in the east.

5. A Roman consul (157–86 BC).

BIOGRAPHICAL NOTE

Leonardo was born in 1452, in the small Tuscan town of Vinci, near Florence. The son of a wealthy Florentine notary and a peasant woman, from an early age he demonstrated considerable social and intellectual skill. From about 1466 he was an apprentice to Andrea del Verrocchio, one of Italy's leading painters and sculptors. There he developed his various artistic techniques, working on religious paintings, and marble and bronze sculptures.

In 1478 Leonardo left Verrocchio to work independently, and then, in 1482, he entered the service of the Duke of Milan. Whilst there he worked as both an architect and engineer, and produced what are now some of his most famous drawings and paintings. His masterpiece, *The Last Supper*, was produced between 1495 and 1497. In 1502 he returned to Florence, and it was here that he painted various portraits, the only one to survive being *Mona Lisa* (1503–6). From there he became court painter to Louis XII of France who was at that time residing in Milan, and for the next few years he divided his time between Milan and Florence, concerned principally with engineering projects and scientific experiments. In 1516 he travelled to France to enter the service of Francis I, where he remained until his death in 1519. As an artist and scientist, Leonardo has had untold influence on all aspects of learning, and is considered to be one of the greatest minds in history.

J.G. Nichols is a poet and translator. His published translations include the poems of Guido Gozzano (for which he was awarded the John Florio prize), Gabriele D'Annunzio, Giacomo Leopardi, and Petrarch (for which he won the Monselice Prize).

HESPERUS PRESS – 100 PAGES

Hesperus Press, as suggested by the Latin motto, is committed to bringing near what is far – far both in space and time. Works written by the greatest authors, and unjustly neglected or simply little known in the English-speaking world, are made accessible through new translations and a completely fresh editorial approach. Through these short classic works, each little more than 100 pages in length, the reader will be introduced to the greatest writers from all times and all cultures.

For more information on Hesperus Press, please visit our website: **www.hesperuspress.com**

To place an order, please contact:
Grantham Book Services
Isaac Newton Way
Alma Park Industrial Estate
Grantham
Lincolnshire NG31 9SD
Tel: +44 (0) 1476 541080
Fax: +44 (0) 1476 541061
Email: orders@gbs.tbs-ltd.co.uk

SELECTED TITLES FROM HESPERUS PRESS

Gustave Flaubert *Memoirs of a Madman*

Alexander Pope *Scriblerus*

Ugo Foscolo *Last Letters of Jacopo Ortis*

Anton Chekhov *The Story of a Nobody*

Joseph von Eichendorff *Life of a Good-for-nothing*

Mark Twain *The Diary of Adam and Eve*

Giovanni Boccaccio *Life of Dante*

Victor Hugo *The Last Day of a Condemned Man*

Joseph Conrad *Heart of Darkness*

Edgar Allan Poe *Eureka*

Emile Zola *For a Night of Love*

Daniel Defoe *The King of Pirates*

Giacomo Leopardi *Thoughts*

Nikolai Gogol *The Squabble*

Franz Kafka *Metamorphosis*

Herman Melville *The Enchanted Isles*

Charles Baudelaire *On Wine and Hashish*

William Makepeace Thackeray *Rebecca and Rowena*

Wilkie Collins *Who Killed Zebedee?*

Théophile Gautier *The Jinx*

Charles Dickens *The Haunted House*

Luigi Pirandello *Loveless Love*

Fyodor Dostoevsky *Poor People*

E.T.A. Hoffmann *Mademoiselle de Scudéri*

Henry James *In the Cage*

Francesco Petrarch *My Secret Book*

André Gide *Theseus*

D.H. Lawrence *The Fox*

Percy Bysshe Shelley *Zastrozzi*